CATCHING CUPID

How to find the love of your life!

Trish McNamara

Cupid Press
Phoenix, AZ

ISBN 0 9673112 0 9
Library of Congress Cataloging-in-Publication Data
McNamara, Trish 1950-
Catching Cupid: How to find the love of your life!
Trish McNamara. - 1st ed.
1. Relationships. I. Title
307.6

Published by
Cupid Press
1009 East Hatcher Road

Phoenix, Arizona 85020

First printing August 2000. *All names and places have been changed to protect the privacy of the individuals.*

Cover illustration by Nina Berkson.

Attention: Study groups, institutions and other organizations: Quantity discounts are available for bulk purchases of this book for education purposes. For information please contact Cupid Press, 1009 East Hatcher Road, Phoenix Arizona 85020. (623) 434-1679, fax (623) 582-3171. E-mail trish@cupidpress.com. Web site www.cupidpress.com.

CATCHING CUPID

ACKNOWLEDGMENTS

Thanks to my many friends and clients for the contributions they've made to this work. Without their open-heartedness and open-mindedness, many truths could not have been revealed. They have been a constant source of information and have provided the push for creative problem-solving.

I would like to express my special gratitude to my editor, Dr. Julie Miller, whose editorial suggestions showed remarkable sensitivity and depth of knowledge. She could see the big picture while keenly fine-tuning the little details.

Many thanks to Linda Browne Putnam, who organized the promotion process and offered her sage advice and enthusiasm.

Thanks to Paul Dagostino of P.D. Productions, Inc., for typesetting the book, and to Mike Ziffer for his editorial assistance and proofreading.

This book is dedicated to my best friend, advocate and husband, Jack Chisum, who paved the road to my understanding of what it means to have the *love of my life.*

TABLE OF CONTENTS

INTRODUCTION

Many women are in an unproductive **DATING CYCLE** and do not realize it! When a relationship ends, they find themselves in mourning. This "time out" can take weeks, months, even years. They re-enter the "dating scene" without any game plan. All they know is that the next situation must be different from the last. This makes dating miserable. Soon they latch on to the very first man who seems interested in them. Next, casting uncertainty aside, they turn this situation into a full-time partnership. Anything seems better than having to "get out there" to meet more men. Yet this new relationship turns out poorly. It ends and the cycle begins again.

It's time to stop this unproductive *dating cycle* before more time elapses in your life. It is time to go for what you really dare to wish for!

The purpose of this book is to coach you in finding the love of your life. Whether you want a boyfriend, life mate, husband or partner, it directs you towards the most dynamic partnership possible. This book outlines a proactive approach to obtaining this goal.

"Catching Cupid" creates an easy, fast way to succeed toward your goal in the most comfortable manner possible. You will spend time developing a "shopping list" of characteristics of the man you wish for. As greater clarity develops, better and faster results occur! When you meet up with the love of your life, there is an **added benefit!** Not only is he recognizable as your perfect partner, but he may be more suited to you than you had ever hoped for.

It just takes one short second to change your destiny, yet what do you do while you continue to search? This book can help you **deal with the dating and waiting game.**

How do you date with confidence? How do you date without experiencing burnout? How do you not get emotionally battle-scarred from time in the trenches? Several chapters are dedicated to dating in the new millennium. You will find systems to set up that make **dating foolproof and even fun!**

Sometimes the most confusing relationship is one that is going nowhere. Learn how to identify relationship pitfalls and avoid them in the future. "Catching Cupid" provides you with homework and asks thought-provoking questions that arm you with information to **jump-start you on the road to finding the most perfect partnership for life.**

Inside, you will find an entire chapter outlining outside sources of help. Once you commit to your goal, there are small miracles that occur to get you where you want to go. Yes, you need to get out there, so **serendipity** can occur.

One of the best things about the book is the many true stories about how people have met. These provide **hope** for the future. **People of all ages have found the love of their lives by getting organized, getting out of mediocre relationships, shaking things up and having a clear set of qualifications.** By getting a concrete agenda, amazing feats can be accomplished. You will become energized from their inspiring tales.

This manual grants you permission, clears the path, organizes the process and gets you inspired to accomplish your goal. Your perfect partner is out there, so why waste any more time! After reading this book, you will be ready to take Cupid's bow in your hands and drive the arrow home.

I know because it happened to me! From observation, information gathering, interviews and much trial and error, I forged my way towards my goal. I have studied this topic for over a decade. When I walked down the church aisle at 47, I felt like I had won the relationship jackpot!

My only regret on this journey was the anxiety about myself. "Was I doing all the right things? Was it O.K. to take a break?" or "Should I give up?" I needed a levelheaded counsel at my feet. What I could have used was a guidebook, similar to the Girl Scouts Handbook. A resource to show me what to do, where to go, and how to stay on track. Most of all, I wanted something straightforward, a comprehensive reference book, one that I could understand without a lot of psychobabble. Ideally, I could refer back to it when the going got tough. I could have saved myself countless hours of self -doubt and self-sabotage had I been able to pick up such a book and fast -tracked to the particular section dealing with whatever overwhelmed me. That is why I have created "Catching Cupid" for you! ***My greatest wish is for you to meet your perfect mate in the shortest, easiest, happiest manner possible.***

Yes, I know that you are almost too frustrated to even admit that this is the one goal you long for, yet seem to never grasp! This book gives you the O.K. plus a road map to guide you along the path to finding the love of your life. And yes, I know that you are stressed about the dynamics of searching and dating. There is a **joyful, spiritual approach to this journey.**

Magic does happen while you are working away. When you start paying closer attention to your world, amazing things happen! The universe seems to kick in and add extra elements to your life. This book engages you to take notice of the small miracles that are around you every day. These small steps will then take you into new directions which hold the surprises that you seek.

This system will get results. This is not a cute route to nabbing a rich husband, but an in-depth, hands-on, sweat equity approach to identifying a "perfect match" for you. ***The definition of "perfect" encompasses a partner that suits YOUR personality, YOUR needs, YOUR lifestyle and YOUR PLANS FOR TOMORROW.*** There is a way to tailor-make the outcome to perfectly match today's you, yet grow along with you into the changes in the future.

Before you can get what you want in a "great" relationship, you must be able to answer some basic yet essential questions. These soul-penetrating questions need to be reflected on. This is the type of "hard work" that the book demands. These answers will unravel issues that are impairing your progress.

Although I want you to take the pace that best suits you, ***the sooner you get started, the better!*** You may want to work in partnership with a friend or organize a study group. The book is formatted for this type of exchange. It will be easy to stay focused. ***The synergy generated by such a gathering of like-minded women is powerful!***

I CHALLENGE YOU to read the chapters and thoughtfully, answer the questions, create time to do the HEARTWORK assignments and make life an adventure while you wait for that serendipitous moment when YOU MEET YOUR PERFECT PARTNER!

With this in mind, let's get started!

"Until one is committed, there is hesitancy,
the chance to draw back, always ineffectiveness.
Concerning all acts of initiative - and creation -
there is one elementary truth, the ignorance of
which kills countless ideas and splendid plans;
that the moment one definitely commits oneself,
then Providence moves too.
All sorts of things occur to help one that would
otherwise never have occurred.
A whole stream of events issues from the decision,
raising in one's favor all manner of unforeseen
incidents and meetings and material assistance, which no man could have dreamt would
have come his way. I have learned a deep
respect for one of Goethe's couplets:

*'Whatever you can do, or dream you can...
begin it. Boldness has genius, power and
magic in it. Begin it now.'"*

W. N. Murray, The Scottish Himalayan Expedition

Part I.
ON YOUR MARK...Getting Clear

"Wisdom is knowing when you can't be wise."

Paul Engle, *Poems in Praise,* 1959

Chapter One

FOCUS, NOT HOCUS POCUS

"All changed, changed utterly."
W. B. Yeats, 1865-1939 (1921)

This book has been created to grant you a WISH! It is designed for those women who are about ready to give up on finding the love of their life. It is also for those who are about to settle for second best. Read these pages and do the exercises and then rethink your direction.

Now is the time of YOUR LIFE! What if you could have the one thing that seems to be eluding you? What if you could have that great relationship? Is that a worthy goal? Absolutely!

Before we dive in, let's make sure that there are no hidden obstacles that will sabotage your progress. Why? Because you need to commit to finding the love of your life and you have to stick with it!

You owe it to yourself, to owe it to yourself.

Keep in mind that seemingly overwhelming obstacles occur to give us an opportunity to learn. The more information one gains while seeking a great relationship, the better the relationship will turn out. We learn the most from actual experience. So some soul-searching is needed to reflect on the past. This is the start of a beautiful partnership!

Roadblocks to that great relationship?

Turn your thinking around regarding how to go about looking for the love of your life. At first, this will feel like writing with your left hand if you are right-handed. This method will take a whole new approach to finding a loved one. Instead of working harder, you will have more fun because you will be thinking, observing and listening in a different manner. You will get what you really want. The perfect relationship will arrive after you have worked out some of the mental kinks and are willing to take some risks.

Do you realize that there are very few things in your life that you want that you don't have or are currently working for? Generally speaking, if you do not have "it," you have decided "it" wasn't worth owning. This "been there and done that" mentality applies to careers, houses, cars, friendships and so on. That one missing element is the one that seems to elude our grasp, that of the meaningful, long-term relationship.

One interesting aspect of my hunt was my relentless faith that there was somebody out there for me. I look back on that aspect of my personality and realize that somehow, even when I was a young girl, I just knew that a great relationship would come to me. However, I had not planned on that "someday" being when I was in my forties! In hindsight, this age now seems appropriate to take on such a long-term commitment. Perhaps my maturity had finally caught up with my faith! Where this unfaltering faith came from, I've also wondered about. I believe it to be a combination of inner knowing and the actual desire or unflinching determination that I had to have a great relationship.

Do you have that unstoppable inner knowing that you will have a great relationship?

What is stopping you?

Take some time to check on your commitment level. Can you stand on your conviction that you will have a perfect partner? Have you forgotten that this is true? Now is the time to stop saying "What if I never find my perfect mate?" and start affirming "It is going to happen at any minute." Why do we not trust timing? In so many other processes of our lives, the timing in hindsight was perfect. We must keep in mind that "time" is really not the enemy but the miracle component. So this changes the "What if" to "When will this happen?"

HEARTWORK: THE BIG QUESTION. "I KNOW THAT I WANT A GREAT RELATIONSHIP, BUT SOMETHING IS STOPPING ME."

Why have you lost hope? Take some reflective time and find out where this inner hope and inner knowing is hidden. Has it been lost, forgotten, or simply mislaid? You can go no further until you have regained that unflinching knowing that you will have a great relationship. Write in the lines below: What is stopping you from going all out to get the relationship that you want?

____

____

It is essential for you to get rid of any roadblocks to your goal. You must become invincible in the knowledge that you can and will get that wonderful relationship. You must know that it is your right to go for it. You have had the "knowing" before, so now get it back. Find a way to gather assurances. It might be seeing every optimistic and romantic movie out there. I loved to watch "When Harry Met Sally" and "Best Friends." It might be spending time with friends who do have great relationships. It is reaffirming that great relationships are out there and surviving.

Seek out people in great relationships and hang out with them. Seeing is believing.

Now is the time to reflect on other areas of life where you have been unflinching about getting something. What about the time you knew you would be a cheerleader, you would graduate from college or would get that interesting job? Conjure up that imagery and that unstoppable feeling. See yourself in a great relationship. What are you doing, where are you going, what are you talking about, what are you feeling and what are you knowing?

Reconnect with that inner knowing.

Many females decide to go it alone and forget the foolishness of relationships altogether. Some became workaholics, blocking out any free time to supersede the loneliness with fatigue. Some turn into swinging bachelorettes and date constantly, without stopping long enough to get in touch with their hearts. Others quietly endure relationships that are not great. Still others take on motherhood as if running a Fortune 500 corporation.

It is never out of style to seek a meaningful partnership.

As I bounced philosophies around and pondered the questions of relationships, I experienced moments of self-loathing. I felt guilt and embarrassment at being so fixed on such a silly notion. After all, this need to have a man in one's life was outdated. Hadn't women been able to have children without even mention of the sperm donor? What had all those women's liberation guidelines been for, if not to experience freedom from the archaic notion of marriage? Why waste all that glorious time looking and seeking when I should be celebrating? Had I not witnessed many miserable marriages that left me feeling sick and sorry for the woman? Had I not felt the excruciating pain of betrayal, sabotage, shock and mental abuse at the ending of my first marriage? Was it not true that I had broken hearts along the way, when I was the one who did not want the relationship? Finally, I wasn't always the easiest person to live with. What was I thinking?

Seek what makes your heart zing.

Even with all this, I still would return to the same sweet song, "Where is my perfect mate?" Ignore the psychobabble of the week. Human beings function best in an alliance with another human being. It is absolutely O.K. to pursue a dream of having a perfect partner. Don't listen to others who have decided NOT to pursue having a partner for themselves. You may feel like a little mouse when you try to argue back that this really is what you want. Just smile and move on, trying not to hear what others are saying. It is best not to even get any of their negative words into your head. Have an excuse ready and hurry away. Create a quick comeback to say to them out loud or in your head. It could go like this: "We need to pursue whatever makes our heart jump."

Do not mix their negative viewpoints into your brain. You must stay positive about your goal. You can not slip into negativity. Why? Negative phrases will jump out at you during times of doubt. Usually around three in the morning, when you wake up in a sweat and just know that your bed will always be empty. You need to have a positive mantra to repeat. Try these affirmations to stay focused:

"I always get what I really desire."
"The universe has a much better handle on the timing of life's events than I do."
"I trust in the universe to grant my wishes when the timing is perfect."
"I grant myself permission to go for the thing that I want most in life...a meaningful relationship."

Now that you have clarified your desire, you need to seek the means of motivation.

Are you clear about your motivation?

This is the time to set and confirm your goal. The key to goal setting is to know your destination. It is not just a matter of knowing the goal. You must understand the reason WHY this goal is important. Then the motivation becomes the fuel to get you there. Are you clear about the reasons why you want such a goal, and are you willing to pay the consequences? Take time to evaluate this goal. Is it at too high of a premium for you? Will it take too much time, cost too much money, or be too scary? If you know why you want something, then you will not be led off track while you go for it. Are you willing to pay the price?

HEARTWORK: WRITE OUT YOUR GOAL.

It has been said that a goal not written down is merely a wish. This is your life and you can have anything that you want. Get out a thick black felt pen and fill in the blanks below.

"I want to find the love of my life because:

____

____

____

Take some time to reflect on other goals that you sought and won. List three previous victories.

These victories can be large or small. List things like quitting smoking, learning a foreign language, changing a career or having a baby.

____

____

____

HEARTWORK: NOW FOCUS ON WHAT THE ROADBLOCKS MIGHT BE IN GETTING THE LOVE OF YOUR LIFE.

Can you write out what some of the "TRADEOFFS" MIGHT BE?

____

____

An example might be: "Since I want to obtain the goal of having a relationship, I will give up many nights when I want to go home and curl up with a good book, especially Friday nights when I'm tired. Instead of agreeing with the 'men are awful' talks, I will stick out my neck and say, 'There are many wonderful men out there.'"

Let's get perfectly clear about the word "perfect."

When I speak of "perfect" as in "the perfect relationship," I do not mean an unattainable goal. "Perfect" is used in the sense that the partnership will be whole, good, pure, absolute, smooth and loving. It seems made just for you. This kind of mutually "perfect" alliance enriches your life. In this committed state, you can grow and pursue your dreams, while living in a state of love, support and harmony. Will every day and hour be perfect? No way! The perfection lies in the alliance with another that enables you to be the best you can be. Yes, you deserve a vital, nurturing, loving, long-term partnership...one that grows, deepens and enriches with time. That can be defined as perfect!

It is a worthy goal to seek the person who soothes the deepest recesses of our soul.

Make an agreement with your heart that this goal is your unalienable right. Let your heart be your sounding board for re-verification. Do not let others pull you from your goal. While you seek your goal, you can't lose sight of that inner knowing that your desire of having a great relationship will be realized! Your soul has always known this, but society has re-prioritized the yearning. Remember that you must have your feet on solid ground, your eyes aimed forward and your mind on the target to reach the bull's-eye.

You have now committed to your goal. You are going to find the love of your life. Remember: a goal is worthless until an action plan is started. The next chapters will prepare you and initiate your personal action plan.

What if you got exactly what you really, really wanted? What if you got exactly what you really, really wanted and many other things that were more than you had ever thought possible?

The journey has begun! Turn to the next chapter, entitled *"Getting Your Footing."* It's time to get rid of any negative issues and fears that can be silently keeping you from your goal of finding a "perfect partner."

Chapter Two

GETTING YOUR FOOTING

"No passion so effectively robs the mind of all its powers of acting with reasoning as fear."

Edmund Burke 1729-97 "On the Sublime & Beautiful (1757)

Your goal is established. Now you must start the journey of unveiling any hidden myths that may impede progress. Before you are really ready, you need to deal with three questions. They will seem rather vague and simple at first. The trick is that each one holds a mountain of issues and core beliefs. By understanding your response to these issues, you will erase areas that are likely to sabotage your progress of finding the love of your life. If you are able to answer YES to all of them, then the work ahead will be easy.

If you answer NO to any one of the questions below, then you need to stop. You then need to work on making a change. Behind the no's are important thoughts, backlogs, and negativity. Although you may attract a relationship, it will never reach the potential to sustain it in a "perfect" way. You may need to seek professional counseling and do some soul-searching before you proceed.

While looking forward into the future, the past held inside can be the unforeseen roadblock.

It is important to take some time out and be able to emphatically say "yes" to all three questions. These are the foundations to achieving your goal. As in archery, you need to double-check your footing (foundation) and your grip (self-esteem) in order to grasp the bow and arrow for a perfect hit.

THE THREE MAJOR QUESTIONS TO YOUR FOUNDATION FOR A GREAT RELATIONSHIP

Do you know that you deserve a good relationship?
Take out a pen and carefully fill in the information below.
The first question is:

1. Do you know in your heart of hearts that you deserve a relationship?

Yes__________ No__________

Not just an average relationship, but one that is really great and will last long into the future. This means that you deserve, merit, have earned, and are entitled to the right to a wonderful relationship.
These are the reasons why I deserve a great relationship:

____

____

____

The second question is:
2. Do you really like men?

Yes__________ No__________

Not just generally but specifically, how do you feel about the men in your life, family and work, and the men you mingle with on a daily basis? Do you have some great male friends? How do you feel about the men in your past? Do you still feel they are fine human beings, or some odd species that you will never be able to understand? Fill in the spaces below.

____

____

____

What is the first thing that comes to mind when completing these statements?

A."Men are___________________________________.

"My last man friend (husband, boyfriend) was a____ person."

C. "You know how men are; they

____

____

____

What is this telling you? Do you like men enough to know that one is worth spending the rest of your life with? Do you see men like you see women - some great, some good, and some needing a little work? Are you realistic in your assessment of men? By looking at your attitude about men, you might be able to locate any area that is holding you back from having a great relationship. For example, if you think that men are "only out to take advantage of women," then you need to stop. Look clearly at the kinds of men you have been attracting. It is mandatory that you be positive.

The third question is:

3. Are you willing to spend the time and effort to validate your wish for a perfect relationship?

Yes__________ No__________

Are you willing to do the work that it takes to acquire this relationship because it is that important to you? Are you willing to spend the time, money, and the energy to stay focused and optimistic about this project? Are you even willing to take the risk of giving up a mediocre relationship?

"Finding a perfect relationship is worth my time because

____

____

It is essential to commit time and energy to obtaining your goal. If you just whine about "not having a relationship" yet do not exert yourself, you are at cross-purposes. There is energy created when you target a goal, are unflinching about why you want it, and commit energy to obtaining it. **The more clear you become, the more energy will magically appear.**

Do you deserve the love of your life?

Many women want a relationship but are unwilling to find out what is blocking them. They are unwilling to WORK at it. They don't want to spend their time and money on unclogging the blockage to a great partnership. They simply want to pout about it.

Many women with incredible incomes won't spend a dime on counseling or going to a singles service. It's time to stop griping, and to start spending money on what you truly want in life. Have you lost track of what you want in life? Why you are working so hard? Are you afraid of spending money on yourself to get what you want? Would a great relationship make you happy? Do you expect this to magically happen?

The important information is about letting YOURSELF HAVE WHAT YOU WANT IN LIFE!

HEARTWORK: GIVE TO THE CHARITY OF CHOICE...Y.O.U.

Take a look at this last month in your life. List all of the time, money and energy that you spent giving to others. Then look at the time it takes to get that time, money and energy. What have you given BACK to yourself?

"There is only one success - to be able to spend your life in your own way."
Christopher Mobley

It is time to address the issue of discovering what makes you happy. Set aside some time to create the steps toward that goal. In this way, when you are planning your month and looking at the calendar, you will prioritize all activities that enhance your steps to your goal. It need not be every weekend. Carefully select a few key places and events that may get you closer to your goal.

You will need to have a few minutes of unplanned moments each week. This keeps you flexible to any new experience that may come up. Isn't it funny that in our highly scheduled life there are so few moments of joy and freedom? We have almost become slaves to the things that have been created to "free up" our lives - the date book, the home gym, the computer, even the car. All of these have been created to give us more time to play, yet they tend to keep us isolated, and the free time never seems to appear. This must be why so many people today complain about being tired.

In writing why you deserve a great partnership, I hope you were able to say what a great person you are. Often when one is frustrated at not having that "great" relationship, nasty thoughts can race through one's head. When a relationship did not work for me, I would hear a loud voice in my head. It went like this; "*Well, you are simply are not tall enough, smart enough, tan enough (left over from the '60s), or thin enough." As the years went on, I added, "Professional enough, rich enough, attractive enough."*

Enough is enough, already! One day, after wallowing in this awful self-deprecating stuff, I realized that "it" was wearing me down. That was the day I put that voice to sleep. If rejections were going to come, fine - but I did not need them from myself too!

HEARTWORK: EXCHANGE THE NO'S FOR THE PRO'S

Now is the time to set aside the time for what you want. You must believe that you are worthy of getting the goal of a "perfect" relationship. What negatives are running around in your head? Prove them wrong with a positive true statement about yourself. Write it in the space provided.

Example: *"I am tall enough, 5'6" is fine and what does height have to with attraction anyway?"*

"I am smarter than I ever thought, and smart in many ways - not just robotic information."

"In summary, I deserve a great relationship because I am all of the above, and more:

Do you really like men?

Often we hear other people's voices answering this question in our head. We need to sort these voices out. You may hear your grandmother saying, "All men are good-for-nothings." Now is the time to focus on reprogramming anything that is not your authentic voice. You will be amazed at all the data stored up in there that is really not what you actually believe in. You may hear a friend's voice saying, *"Why do you need a relationship anyway? Haven't you got everything you need already? Men are just a waste of time."* Spend time on knowing why you are ready for this lifetime commitment, why you deserve it and how you really enjoy spending time with men. Before you can move forward, do some mental housecleaning of the old way your mind dealt with these issues.

HEARTWORK: The Brain Unsizzler

Write out all the little evil snakes in your head. These are the squiggly, wiggly little voices that are sabotaging your efforts to getting exactly what you desire. Think of your head like a poster for Medusa - the woman with snake hair. What are all those negative messages that are swimming around, telling you that your goal of a perfect mate is silly, that men are not worthy, and that looking for a perfect relationship is not worth your time and energy?

"I believe that looking for a perfect relationship is worthy of my time and energy because

---

Are you willing to spend the time and effort to validate your wish for a perfect relationship?

You are responsible for your own happiness. If you do not have what you want in life, there is a reason. It could be that you are full of mixed messages or self-doubt, won't spend the time, money or energy, or have not stopped and really focused on this goal. Now is the time to create a goal for yourself and go for it. Time is moving by. Give yourself the present that you have always wanted most for yourself - a meaningful, loving, supportive and advocating relationship. You need to prioritize and order your INTENTIONS.

I've found out an interesting phenomenon. Our loved ones friends and coworkers sometimes block our growth by accident. They mix our agendas with their "stuff." They can not perceive our dreams like we do. As women, we ask permission to have our dreams. If we do not get a joyous permission slip, then we often feel invalidated and forgo our wishes. This is why we must have a strong clarification that creates an internal O.K. and we can then proceed. What is really funny, though, is that when we do obtain our dreams, those same people are the first to say, *"I knew you could do it!"*

My aunt is a great example of a gal who goes for it. She has always led an adventurous life with a steady self-confidence that has taken her all over the world and towards many unusual and interesting careers. Her story is about getting clear about intentions and listening to your own self-counsel.

After her husband's death, she quickly took over his consulting firm. Her close friends told her she could not do it. They believed she should not even attempt to keep it going. Yet she knew inside that she had to give it a try. So, although she was totally unfamiliar with this career and still in shock from his sudden death, she jumped in with her usual vigor. During one of her trips to Asia, she realized how lonely she was for some companionship. In most of the places she visited, she did not speak the language.

When she reached the Regency Hotel in Hong Kong, she craved a simple "hello" and "how's the weather?" kind of a chat in English. She realized that she had not had a real conversation in English for over three weeks. Another insight was her need to have a good relationship. As she was heading for a table in the dining room, something stopped her in her tracks. It was a man in a pair of gray flannel pants, penny loafers, and a navy blue blazer. Since this man was reading The New York Times, she knew he could speak English. She did not hesitate for more than a second. She asked if he would care if she joined him for breakfast. He said, "Please do." They were married the following year. As usual, when she made her mind up for a new adventure, it materialized rapidly.

When you are ready, you can start, but you can't give up!

Today is the day to mark as the beginning and keep moving forward. You need to stick to your intentions. You can now tell people about your goal. Just like apartment hunting, the more people you know and the more people you tell, the more rapidly you will find a new place.

Many years ago my mother and I had a conversation about the idea of LUCK. She had just read an article entitled "Lucky People" in Reader's Digest. It investigated those people whom we consider "lucky." Surprisingly, they were not extraordinary in any way but one. They had lots of friends, belonged to many organizations, knew lots of people and, during the course of a week, talked to many, many people. Their "luck" was the outcome of telling lots of people just what they were needing and the network coughing up just the right thing. This is the kind of luck you will need to cultivate. ***Get out and get lucky!***

Fix the past

The biggest enemy to getting what you want in life is YOU. So many times, the first thing out of a single woman's mouth is something negative about the opposite sex. This acts as self-sabotage when looking for a mate. If you have had difficult relationships, with unreasonable or abusive men, then you need to seek professional help. Take time out to heal these wounds or you may keep attracting men with similar disorders.

You need to heal the past. You must forgive your past relationships regardless of the amount of grief you experienced. Move through this by realizing that these individuals did not have the tools at the time to change their behavior. Reconfigure the past and realize that you learned a lot about what you DO want for the future. View your past partnerships as good - but the love, the learning and the common goals changed along the way.

Remember, you do not have to be "perfect" to have a relationship. Just love. You need to be loving and willing to love.

Now that you have gotten yourself established on solid ground, there are a few things that can still be holding you up. Chapter Three is called *"Closing the Barn Door."* It deals with tackling the issues around closure.

Chapter Three

CLOSING THE BARN DOOR

"A woman has got to love a bad man once or twice in her life to be thankful for a good one."
Marjorie Kinnar Rawlings

You've committed to the goal of seeking your "perfect" mate. Now that you find yourself on solid ground, let's look back at some of your past relationships. What have you learned from them? Is there anything left to be cleaned up from the past?

To acquire that "great" relationship, the old relationships need to be carefully put to rest. If true closure has not occurred, resentment, anger, hate and regret hold you back. Or the opposite can occur - each new relationship seems dim compared to one from the past. We have a tendency to place the lost relationship on the level with the devil or with the saints. Either way, this makes finding a replacement impossible. So the good, the bad and the ugly past can hold up progress. It is now time to reach CLOSURE.

Why? Because old unresolved issues can hinder and delay our search for the perfect mate.

Closure is your message to the universe that you are confident that the future contains good stuff!

The degree of anger, self-accusation and strain left from all the life-affecting decisions that surround a breakup can take a toll. The steps of grieving are needed to process through any breakup, divorce or ending. Even meeting somebody new who is wonderful yet it does not work out, can leave a negative impression. We can feel pain and regret even when the decision is mutual. Any relationship that did not work out for any reason can feel destructive. It must be clearly processed and closed. Only then can one easily move forward.

Blindly close a door behind you, knowing another will open.

At 29, Lilly was busy raising her four kids under the age of eight. Since her husband's death, she had grieved for a short period but her life was amazingly busy and full. She felt sorry for her friend

Gale. Gale had called crying; she was divorced with a young son. She wanted to get out and meet people but she was shy and did not know where to go. After Lilly hung up, she remembered something she had glanced at in the church bulletin. It was an announcement about a Parents Without Partners meeting. She called Gale back and said she would drive them if Gale could hunt up a sitter that could handle their five kids. They made it to the meeting. Both met nice and interesting men. Lilly was the most surprised and delighted. She met her future husband there. He was a widower with two children. It didn't take a long for their combined households to mesh and move right along. It's amazing what can happen when you take a little time out for yourself!

Many of us will see years pass before we actually are ready to do battle again. Often we are the last one to really know that we are not ready. By doing the exercises below, the grief process will shorten, allowing you to get back to dating sooner - thus speeding up the process of finding the love of your life.

One sure way to sabotage your own efforts is by comparing each new encounter with the old one and never giving the new man a fresh start. This is a sign that the anger, disappointment, disruption and sense of loss from that past relationship is not totally healed. If you find yourself constantly thinking about the "old relationship" instead of getting ready for and excited about a new one, then action needs to be taken.

Here is a quick quiz to check on your current closure status.

THE CLOSURE QUIZ:

❑ 1. Do you find yourself waiting by the phone and checking your messages for a possible reprieve from Mr. X?

❑ 2. Do your friends start rolling their eyes and grabbing their cell phones as you launch into yet another whining session about the departed Joe Cool?

❑ 3. Does every activity have a sort of gray pallor to it because the last time you were there you experienced this with Mr. Wonderful? (And these may range from getting your car washed to doing your income tax.)

❑ 4. Have you started to have the paper delivered to your home to check the obituaries, the marriage announcements and marriage application columns to see if he has been able to move on - so that you can?

Grief

Putting the kidding aside, are you totally focused on the future?

Have you processed the stages of grief for each of your past relationships?

Stages of Grief:

Shock
Denial
Anger
Self-recrimination
Forgiveness
Ability to move forward

These steps need to be processed for all of your past significant relationships. You may find that a relationship from the far past is actually the one holding up your progress. Each step of the process needs to be acted on.

So line up the troops for inspection. This is the Autopsy of Boyfriends Past. Just as is done in very mysterious deaths, or in solving a great mystery, one needs to exhume these bodies for a final look at what killed them. Take a look at your relationships from the past. Stop and view this person to learn what may help you in your next relationship. Take a non-emotional vantage point and view the old relationship for any possible CLUES to its demise. Look for possible traces of poison or foul play, and pinpoint the time of death. Be an Inspector Poirot and get the FACTS. The method a detective adapts is to fill in the missing facts to substantiate the REASON for death. The skill comes by not jumping to a conclusion before all the facts are in. You must let the facts show you the way to the answers. Only after this can you draw your hypothesis.

HEARTWORK: AUTOPSY OF BOYFRIENDS PAST PART I.

Take out a piece of paper. Write these in columns.

Who are the past loves of your life?

1. List them by name.

2. After each name, state the cause of death of the relationship. In other words, what is the real reason that you two did not make it for the long haul?

A list could read something like this:

Joe . . . . .Perpetual bachelor
Tom . . . . .Too serious
Karl . . . . .Went back to wife
Sam . . . . .Too uptight

3. Now that that is done, look at what was gained by these untimely

deaths. It is important to note that the reasons for the breakups never have anything to do with you being an inferior person. It always relates to problems that have to do with his agenda and yours. There is little need to beat yourself up over these issues. Self-recrimination evaporates when you know that you as a person had little to do with it not working out. Just realize that you did not need to change in any way to have a relationship last. You simply need to find "the right" relationship!

HEARTWORK: AUTOPSY OF BOYFRIENDS PAST PART II

Now take a look at each man and what he has contributed to your life. These characteristics will be applied to THE LIST in Chapter 9, "Working from a List." This information is essential in building a character sketch of what you really value for your future mate. When the information is compiled, it allows you to appreciate the men from the past for the knowledge you gained about yourself and about what you want in your next relationship.

List the same names you did in Part One. This time, focus on their qualities. List each man's greatest traits, worst characteristics, and what you learned by being with him.

Your list might look like this:

Name . . . . .Pete
Greatest Traits . . . .Great energy
Worst Traits . . . . . .Different lifestyle
What I learned . . . .Learned to let somebody love me.

Remember, we need as much information as possible to identify our ideal mate. Do not be afraid to dwell on the sexual, spiritual, physiological and esthetic areas. Think about how you felt. Was there laughter, gaiety and conversation? Were you able to feel like yourself? Was it easy or was there always tension?

This list does many things. One, it gives you closure to see the names written down. Two, you can see that the ending had little to do with you. Three, you can see the progressive addition of qualities that you have now experienced. Four, you can see all the wonderful things that you have learned. Five, you can see that you have survived.

Most of all, an attitude of true optimism will prevail. If after you complete the list, you say, **Hey, if I could roll up all these positive attributes into one perfect guy, then I would really have the man of my dreams! - now you are on the track to Mr. Perfect.**

Stare into the face of anger and you will see fear. Look deeper into fear and you will encounter longing.

One may find that there is still a little hang-up on one particular fella from the list. He seems so much more perfect for you than the rest. You need to take some time out to thank and forgive him for not being able to be in your life. Then convince yourself that there is something else that you need that he cannot provide for you. This particular thing may not be revealed yet. You now need to endorse blind faith that there really is someone that will suit your soul even better. When you have that new relationship, you will be thankful that each and every man on your old list <u>did not</u> turn out to be your one and only. You can have all the good stuff without much bad. Try to celebrate new beginnings and give yourself a pat on the back for all the love, time and energy you have already given to this most important search of a lifetime.

HEARTWORK: ANATOMY OF A BOYFRIEND'S PAST PART III

This third activity will enable you to process the final aspect of closure to forgive and forget.

Get out a separate piece of paper. Write each man's name on a piece of paper and burn it in the fire or over a candle. Or wrinkle it up and throw it into the trash. Or visualize the man and see him accepting your telling him you have forgiven him. Go on a hike and throw the ashes into a valley as if in a cremation ceremony. Take action, really "feel" the forgiveness, and now you can move from the past. As you do this, thank him for all the fun times and all that you have learned for the future. Really work on letting it go. Holding on to the anger will impede your progress. You can not move forward until you reach closure about your past. Keep in mind that all this information is essential in creating your perfect future partner.

"Thanks for the memories and may you rest in peace!"

Why is it important to glean what you can from the past, forgive and move on? **Your energy is sapped If you do not clear up the past.** You do not need to actually get back to the person. You can do it by creating the "closure pictures." Your mind does not know the difference between the actual activity and the mental picture. If you do not create a formal grief time, you may be surprised by attacks of remorse, sorrow and regrets. Here is an example of how the brain is keeping track of things even when you are not. It also gives you a glimpse at the idea of a "style of grieving."

It is very interesting to take a look at your own particular style of grieving when a relationship ends. *I* found that my grieving would come three months after I broke up with the man. At first, when the relationship ended, I felt such a great amount of relief. This gave me a sense of joy. Then when I wasn't even thinking about him, while rolling along with other pursuits, BANG...the sorrow and remorse would set in. This was my "Oh, I made a mistake!" phase. The depression and guilt and remorse would hang heavy over me. I had to go through the grieving process at this time. I also noticed that there would be another hit about a year later. This was triggered by the one-year anniversary of some event we shared. It was only after consulting my date book that I'd realize that a past event was one year old. This time I would be flooded with melancholy memories of the relationship that was now dead. The mind keeps track of our vital information.

HEARTWORK: IS BREAKING UP SO VERY HARD TO DO?

Do you know your breakup pattern? Is it detrimental or healing? Note how much time it takes to break up even a so-so relationship. As the years go by, how many months have been spent in recovery time from past relationships?________________________________.

Yikes! This is scary. The years spent in recovery.

Is there a difference between the ones that broke up with you and those that you decided to break away from? How did you deal with the grief? Did you have to deal with issues of anger, depression, fear or jealousy?

Pain + Time = Recovery

Optimism

One of the drawbacks to the grieving process is the pain. Another is the time spent. This is why you need to unravel the grieving process and fine-tune it. Find clues to relationships that could have been better and those that should never have been. You are on the fast track to finding the love of your life. Your goal is to obtain the "perfect" relationship, without losing so much time and feeling so much pain in the recovery process.

Optimism arises when you know that the "old" did not work because the "new" will be so much better.

Stand back and dissect the past in order to see what is next. This is why the autopsy is so essential. Put on a mask and dig around as objectively as possible to see what was good, what was true and what was bloody awful.

Unfortunately, there is no way to guarantee that pain will never happen. When you arrive at the other side of the process, hopefully you will feel ready to try again. As in childbirth, the memory of pain is quickly diminished by the love of the child. So too, the wonderment of romance and the contentment of companionship will win over the agony of defeat. When you get to the point of thinking that perhaps you will never have another relationship ever again, I know that you are actually ready for a new relationship. This is the halfway step between forgiveness and moving on.

To ponder the future, even with trepidation, is actually a sneak peak into a new set of hopes for tomorrow.

Use the "Autopsy" process from now on, while dating. This will aid in staying optimistic - by understanding that learning occurs with each new encounter.

You have dealt with relationships from your past. Let's look at what you have today. Are you still in a relationship and hoping that it will become "perfect"? Or are you trying to gain the courage to leave it behind? The next chapter, entitled "LETTING GO," will guide you towards clarity on why you should never "settle." It will help you get clear about what you want and help guide you while meeting and dating men.

Chapter Four

LETTING GO

"Wood may remain ten years in the water, but it never becomes a crocodile."
Congolese Proverb on Change

In the last chapter, you let go of old relationships. Now you should be ready to break into new territory. Unless...you are still in a current relationship. If this is true and you are reading this book, it should be obvious that your current situation is not "THE ONE." Also, during the dating process, you may be tempted to enter into one of these situations. Often, the tricky part is letting "it" go. Here are some scenarios that are characteristic of "going nowhere" relationships.

"GOING NOWHERE" RELATIONSHIPS

- ❑ **You** are dating a married man.
- ❑ **You** are in a relationship that is just O.K. or so-so.
- ❑ **You** are in a relationship and still dating other men.
- ❑ **You** are in a relationship for recreational sex.
- ❑ **You** are in a relationship while you shop for another one.
- ❑ **You** are you in a relationship that is going nowhere yet you can not seem to move on?
- ❑ Are you spending most of your time trying to make the relationship work?
- ❑ Are you too tired from all this to think about about moving on?

Why settle for good when you can have GREAT? Why settle?

Some women are thinking, "Should I break up the relationship I now have?" The answer is yes! If you are thinking that it could be better...it can!

Many women are in going-nowhere relationships. They are with men who are simply not good for them. In many cases, these men are not awful, but the circumstances or the chemistry or the future does not look good. If one took a pulse of the situation, it should be placed on the critical list. To put it another way: when it is right, you know it 100%.

Let's be proactive about our own lives and light a match where our heart wants a flame.

You must wake up and make some choices and then take some chances. This is your life and only you can make it the way you want it. Staying with somebody who is not able to aid you in having a great relationship is not a good start to anything. **So if you are in a "going nowhere" relationship, you need to get going**!

Now is the time to snap out of it in order to move towards the one thing that you deserve in life...a meaningful great relationship.

Some may find it difficult to pinpoint the actual reason to flee. Use this list to judge the "kind" of relationship you are in or thinking about entering.

RELATIONSHIP KILLERS: You must move on:

- ❑ if he is verbally or physically abusive.
- ❑ if he is still hung up on his last relationship, finding it hard to release issues from his past.
- ❑ if he is uncertain and unwilling to commit to the future.
- ❑ if it is perfect except for one thing: he is too old, too young, too anything that will not be changing.
- ❑ if he is convenient.
- ❑ if he is always "just there."
- ❑ if he has loads of money and that is about all you have to say about him.
- ❑ if you have a great sex life and that's about it.
- ❑ if he claims he will leave his wife.
- ❑ if you have to make excuses about him to your friends, relatives, colleagues or even to a grocery clerk.
- ❑ if every sentence that you start about him starts with "But he...."
- ❑ if he is not madly, deeply, passionately in love with you.

Then say ***"Adios!"***

Research confirms - **when it is right...it is right.** Both people are ready and know that the other person is perfect for them. There is an inner knowing that is so strong that it is undeniable. Both parties recognize this because of their mutual invincible knowing. Good relationships do not take all of your energy to make it right. Great relationships do not have any excuses.

"Perfect" relationships start wonderfully and stay great. So if the sparkle is listless and the laughter is strained and you are still just dating...get out of it! You must trust that your "perfect" person is out there. Remember, it is obvious to both people when it is "right."

People in a good relationship are busy creating an interesting life. People who are in poor relationships spend much of their time just getting to "normal."

When you are in a good partnership, you experience life with great ease. The two people know that they are meant for each other. They awaken each other's soul, thus creating tremendous personal power. This synergy brings forth the maximum possibility for fulfillment in each person.

This is not a magical fairy tale! A great relationship is available to anyone with the esteem to go for it!

Lea had been dating John for two years. The fact that he was 21 years younger was not a problem. They had every interest in common. He was an architect and she an interior designer. He was so perfect for her except for one detail. HE wanted a family. HER children were just finishing college. For the last year, they had several breakups over this issue. When John left town to pursue a dream job, she was sad. Yet the next day she decided that this was the time to let him go pursue all his dreams. She wrote him a letter and posted it. On the way home she stopped at one of her clients and met the most amazing man. He was an art critic and architecture connoisseur. They had so much to talk about!

When you are clear about letting go and move on wishing the other well, amazing things can happen. **Magic happens when you allow grace and dignity to be your guides.**

Now is the time to commit to the kind of future you want. You can have anything that you desire and you can dream as big as you wish. This is not a time for mediocrity, especially in a relationship. Don't waste time with excuses and procrastination. It is time to get what you want. If you are still unable to act, you will be getting clearer and clearer as you read the book.

HEARTWORK: WHAT FEARS ARE STRINGING YOU ALONG IN A "SO-SO" RELATIONSHIP?

Finish the sentence:

"I am in a so-so relationship because_____________________.

If you are fearful of getting out of the relationship or fearful of being on your own, then you need to face those fears. The psychological reasons have to do with one thing: fear. The "what if's" rule our lives. "What if's" make it impossible to move forward and yet more unbearable to stay in the present. Remember: if something is bothering you, it is not a fluke; it is a real thing that needs to be dealt with. Trust yourself - if the relationship that you are in just doesn't "feel" right, let it go. Information is gained by stepping away.

Battling the "What Ifs"

Often, we do not give ourselves credence to follow our dreams. Here we are living our life and yet not listening to our inner self and finding answers for ourselves. This is your life and you must take risks. Stop wallowing in the "what if's":

THE WHAT IF'S:
What if I never find love?
What if this relationship suddenly improves?
What if I look back and wish I had stayed in an old relationship?
What if I hadn't done this, gone there, learned that?
What if I never feel the same?
What if I end up being a bag lady?

Stop it! When you are in the rest home and reviewing your life, do you want to say, "Well, I decided to settle and marry him and it was an O.K. life"? It is far better to have lived a life of expectation and adventure towards the ultimate goal of a soul mate. Even "I kept looking and never found him" is much better than hanging around for decades waiting for things to change. Remorse will just not cut it in the end. **This is your life - get out there and do something about it.**

Here is the truth - what you expect, you will receive. What you seek, you will find. If you know what you want and stay open, you will get it. Every universal law will prove this again and again. If you want a great relationship and you are clear about it and you get out there to find it and seek it...IT WILL FIND YOU!

HEARTWORK: MY LIFE IS TOO SHORT TO SETTLE NOW.

Fill in the blanks below in order to complete the sentence:

"I, ________________________ (name), agree to stop settling for a mediocre relationship. Life is too short to not forge ahead and seek my most 'PERFECT RELATIONSHIP.' I will not let these fears stop me:

___

___

___

I expect more and deserve more!

Say "no" to mediocrity!

You are the only thing standing in the way of your getting the very best loving relationship that is out there. This is one area of your life that you should want to be more FABULOUS and WONDERFUL than anybody else's. YOU simply need to believe that you can have all that you want. This is the time to administer "tough love." Stop whining, get out there and go for it!

Mediocrity is what really killed the cat.

Still looking while staying in a relationship does not work. You can not shop in one store while you are in another. **Get out and get single.** You can only be available when you are physically, mentally, spiritually, sexually, psychologically and socially obtainable. Being in a less-than-great relationship will sap your energy and your self-esteem.

The most difficult decision to make is when you are in a "just O.K. relationship." A so-so relationship is one that has difficult areas and some good ones too. You are hoping that things will change or that you will get used to the bad stuff. If you are getting by or hoping for change, get out the door! The only person who will be changing is you, and the change might be for the worse. In many cases, the woman takes on some of the "bad" behavior that she had hoped to change. It could be the rage-aholic behavior of the man. Soon she might find herself over the edge and close to becoming the "raging" one. It will only be harder to get out as time passes.

Often, the things that you wish to change end up becoming even more pronounced as the years go by. Look at the elderly in rest homes. People who have been obsessed about money do nothing but fret and worry about money every minute of every day. They do not become less entangled with their issues; rather, they gain a singular focus on them.

When you stay in a relationship that is going nowhere, you mess with your head. You keep trying and nothing changes. You keep trying to fix things and make things better. Slowly (even though you think that you are being very positive about all this) you are becoming pessimistic and negative about life. So the only thing that gets "changed" is your inner spirit. What a waste! So that when you are finally free, you have a rotten attitude and you are worn-out. This is why the "mediocre" relationship is a no-win situation.

Engage yourself before you become "engaged."

Stop the dissertation on how you are too old to find any decent men. They are out there and just as eager to have a meaningful relationship as you are. Even if you are 60, 70 or 80 and you want that perfect partner, he's probably out there. You would not desire it if it was something that could not be fulfilled.

If you are constantly needing assurances from other people, then perhaps you are trying to convince yourself to ignore what is wrong.

If you are in a relationship just for sex or occasional companionship, yet yearn for a "great" relationship - give it up. Wouldn't it be nice if that person had a chance to meet the person of their dreams too? Are you so selfish that you are using (even if it is mutual) the other person to get something that is not essential? It is time to give up the "quick fix" and go for the love of your life.

One of the fears many women have is that of living alone. How many times have we heard a woman say, "Well, I left my parents' house, only to live with my husband." When looking for a new relationship, this woman may be looking in all the wrong places. The first perfect relationship she needs to have is one with herself. Create a healthy person, not a needy, must-fix-this-emptiness woman. If living on your own has been forced upon you by a divorce or death, then you probably need to come to terms with this situation. Only when you enjoy living with yourself can you expect another to enjoy living with you. **If you plan on living "happily ever after," you better start with living happily with yourself.**

Self-kindness

It is never too late to have a heart-to-heart talk with yourself and look at the reality of the situation that you are in. Is the other person in your relationship going to change for you in the ways that will make the relationship work at the optimum level?

Often the greatest act of kindness is to yourself.

Go ahead and get selfish. I decided that if I got one thing right in this lifetime, it would be having a really great relationship. It was then that I realized that I could not and would not stay in any relationship where my gut always felt a little queasy. I knew that I had to keep those wagons moving west. Herd 'em up and head 'em out. A solid loving relationship is really possible.

In the act of saying "no," you are letting the universe know what you do want.

The great relationships start out great! They are great from day one until the end. Very few grow to greatness. If they do, there is a price to pay. Often, by the time the relationship has mellowed, there are issues that are ingrained into the relationship's foundation. Bad habits do not disappear or go away. The couple simply gets used to them. A couple that starts out yelling and arguing don't stop at some juncture. They simply get used to the noise.

If you are in the business of finding a partner for life, shouldn't your standards be very high?

HEARTWORK: WHAT DO YOU WANT, ANYWAY?

Start listing the qualities you desire in a "perfect" relationship. Include things like great communication, respect, fun, laughter and so on. These can be the foundation for "THE LIST." I have dedicated an entire chapter to this task.

___

___

___

Now you have cleaned up the past and the present. You will need some fuel to get out there and start seeking this perfect partner. Chapter 5 walks you through the *"TINY STEPS"* needed to getting what you want.

PART II.
GET SET...Looking around

"The one important thing I have learned over the years is the difference between taking one's work seriously and taking oneself seriously. The first is important and the second disastrous."
Margot Fonteyn

Chapter Five

TINY STEPS

"Tis known by the name of perseverance in a good cause, and of obstinacy in a bad one."
Lawrence Sterne 1713-68 Tristom Shandy (1759-67)

Are you willing to be a fool for love?

The first step is the hardest, they say. One way to help make your search less traumatic is to take very small steps. Even then you will experience fright and disappointment.

Focus on the NOW, not the WHEN and not the THEN.

Reaching the finish line in first place the first time is an impossibility. While searching for the love of your life, how do you keep trying - while still maintaining a positive attitude? How many tries will it take? There is no exact number of tries to guarantee the perfect hit. Can you hear the embarrassment that you subject yourself to as you try and try?

How many times will it take to hit the bull's-eye?

You have clarified your goal, you have reviewed the past, and now is the time to get GOING. This chapter is dedicated to developing FLEXIBILITY and TENACITY while INCREASING YOUR ABILITY TO BOUNCE BACK. These are essential while dating.

As you work toward your goal of a perfect relationship, you must allow yourself to miss the mark. A running coach would have you focus on staying flexible while building the leg muscles. You would be staying loose while building strength and power. The coach would stress getting the form down and then the speed. In dating, this is the evaluating and list-writing time. In sports there are many misses. So too in dating. The way to stay afloat is to take small steps and keep a smile on your face. There must be room for serious laughter. There will be mistakes made! So while letting the level of pride drop, you need to heighten your awareness of life's small miracles.

This is where the focus needs to be. Just remember that some of life's best miracles come in small humorous packages. Do not take yourself too seriously!

Make room for those silly mistakes and mishaps. This could include thinking that you have finally met Mr. Right and telling your best friend. Soon the phone rings and Mr. Right is calling to tell you that he has decided to date his son's friend's mother! Perhaps you are meeting some man for drinks, and as you enter the room, your new shoes slip on the marble floor and down you go. As we enter into new worlds, we are going to take wrong turns. **Yet the more newness we encounter, the more rapidly finesse is developed.**

The seasoned traveler does not necessarily encounter fewer problems; she simply experiences less stress over them.

Obviously, the more opportunities you have, the more rapidly you will increase your chances of hitting the bull's-eye. Luck is the number of opportunities that you come across, not some miraculous event that drops from sky. Those "lucky in love" have gotten out and researched the topic. I**t is important to get out of your tight routine and start exploring new territory.**

Over and over, I have met women who have met their mates after they have moved to a new place or started a new job. Somehow, the change forces them to look around and notice new things. Moving to a new city really shakes things up. You must stay alert and awake because you are out of your comfort zone. You may even have to ask strangers for help and directions. In this new environment, you are really looking and not floating along in your usual trance.

Even leaving town for the weekend can present a new viewpoint. When you return, you see the familiar geography from a new vantage.

Here is a story of a woman who made a decision to move on. She was forced to have an open mind, and by doing so, found the love of her life.

Betsy had been working in New York for over ten years. She had hoped to find a husband and have a family. Yet, all she had been experiencing from her job in advertising was proposals for dates from married men. After a trip to visit her cousin in Colorado, she returned to pack and move there. The day she moved into her new apartment she slipped on the ice. By day two, she found herself in a cast and on her sofa surrounded by boxes. She felt like an utter fool who had made a big mistake in moving. She wanted to cry but couldn't even find the Kleenex. The only person she knew in the entire state was her cousin, and she was going out of town on business. She'd sent over a friend named Brad to help Betsy with the rest of the move. It was hard for Betsy to rely on anyone. She was skeptical of this mountain man. Yet he proved helpful, happy and a refreshing surprise. He helped with food and videotapes and even brought her out for a drive for a change of pace. It only took a few days for her opinion to change. When spring arrived, they took walks in the country. She started loving his world of the mountains and fresh air. They were married six months later.

Betsy displayed flexibility and tenacity. She took a risk and moved to a new place. She validated her wishes for pursuing what she really wanted. She was strong by being flexible.

It just takes one letter to transform "chance" to "change."

How do you feel about making a fool of yourself? This is a real possibility when you are taking risks and seeking change. How many times have we re-looked at a foolish episode in our lives and found it to be one that brought us great pleasure, a powerful life lesson or a wonderful surprise? If the love of your life is not in your life now, then he is out there in the land of the unknown. Can you allow yourself to go on an adventure into the unknown? Are you willing to use the machete and hack your way into the jungle in order to find your lost treasure?

When looking for love, the element of surprise is essential.

So many people met their life mates after mishaps, pitfalls and adventures. People have met in stalled elevators, the wrong class reunion, while driving the wrong way on a one-way street and even in a Halloween costume! A friend met her husband while dressed as a gypsy (with all her jewelry on and most of her rouge). He was in a gorilla costume! Another reconnected with her mate because her mother was processing some papers at city hall. The attorney recognized the last name and asked if her daughter was the one he had dated some 10 years earlier. My aunt met her perfect partner while attending a class entitled "Grieving and Loss." She was adjusting to the loss of her husband of over 50 years, and he was getting over a divorce. The instructor had the class pair off and this unlikely couple (she was in her 60s and he was in his 30s) have been best pals ever since.

What would have happened if these people had been too worried about new things to not go to a party without a date, had not forced themselves to attend a class, or not taken a risk to reacquaint with an old friend?

The time was the early '60s, and Lydia lived in a small, rural Midwestern town. Lydia drove into the gas station to fill her truck with gas. Driving in, she noticed that the apple that she planned to munch on had fallen to the floor of the truck. As she reached for it, the truck lurched forward at full speed. In a few short seconds, she zoomed through the station, crashing into the house that was attached to the garage. Luckily, she was not hurt, but so embarrassed she could barely speak. The gas station attendant rushed over, fearing the worst. At first, she would not look up as he asked her if she was all right. Finally, their eyes locked and he knew she was special. They were married shortly after and are still married 36 years later.

Scheduling new events

So how do we have a man find out about our wonderful selves, anyway? We can't all go around driving into buildings. You never know when the opportunity will come to you, so you need to be alert all the time. You need to break out of the old worried self who walks along and listens to all the inner mumbo jumbo. It's time to look up and out. A random smile and some eye contact are also great. So what if you say the wrong thing, smile for no reason and chat with a perfect stranger in an elevator? You are confirming to everyone that life is good and you are ready for new things.

Each day, allow some time for some unplanned event to take place. If nothing happens, you at least had a great time with yourself.

We are so worried about making a fool out of ourselves or that we won't look busy. This is the time in your life to do just that. Try to be open to new adventure each week. If somebody at work mentions bowling, a sport that you had previously thought of as silly, take a breath and ask if you can tag along. Add this to your new adventures list. Allowing some unstructured time can open up all kinds of new possibilities.

What does it take?

HEARTWORK: ONE NEW PERSON, PLACE OR THING EACH DAY.

I know that you carry a date book or daytimer or have a calendar that rules your life. From now on, I would like you to try to have a new entry each day. Enter any new small or large adventure. They can be silly, dumb or embarrassing. The point is that you lived through it!

The entries might read: *"Drove home a new way, got lost, noticed a cool antique shop, will go on Saturday. Had my hair cut differently. Bought a new leopard purse. Went by myself to that old Mexican restaurant. Met a blind date for drinks. Played foos-ball. Attended a hockey game."*

Keep this up until you meet your perfect mate.

P.S. This homework is one of the few that contains a rule.

RULE: You may not accomplish any of these activities inside your home.

An adventure a day keeps the blues at bay.

There is a way to become really self-confident about taking on new adventures. JUST do it! Start by doing the smallest of things. An example might be taking an earlier bus to work in order to have a muffin and an espresso in a new coffee bar. The more you get out, the better and easier it becomes. I compare this to giving a speech. It takes more than a few times to gain your composure. Yet, soon you will be wondering what you were so fearful of. Practice, practice and more practice.

It is far better to be dumb and lucky than all-knowing and lonely!

LESSONS ON GETTING OUT THERE

LESSON #1 An Eye for an Eye:

When meeting men, what I had a really hard time with was making eye contact. I honestly thought that every time a man looked at me, something was wrong. I would either look to see if my slip was showing or frown at him because I thought he was thinking I was homely. Part of this stemmed from being a child who wore glasses from age 5 on. At that time, very few children wore glasses, and mine were always taped and dirty, and pink or blue with rhinestones. People would look at me probably in pity. I just knew they thought I was an ugly little girl. As an adult, the feeling stayed with me. I had to practice returning the glance with a smile. This was harder to me than learning backhand in tennis.

LESSON #2 Whose Smooth Move:

Once eye contact was made, I had to learn how to be open and let the man make the moves. I worked at coming up with ways to keep the conversation going. I worked at not blushing and looking down. I had to calm down my negative mind. Next, I had to learn not to do everything. Yes, I encouraged the man to talk. Yes, I returned the conversational volley. I just stopped feeling that it was up to me to make the meeting "perfect." Let him worry about all that!

LESSON #3 Relax and Watch the Show:

The more I got out, the more compliments I got, and my self-confidence bloomed. In time, I learned how to sit back and just let things happen. Soon all the "work" left the equation and I just enjoyed "getting out" to simply people-watch. Believe me, I was never disappointed!

OPTIMISM: *The doctrine that this world is the best possible world, and that the good of life overcomes the bad. An inclination to put the most favorable construction upon actions and happenings, or anticipate the best possible outcome.*

(Webster's New Collegiate Dictionary)

Do you want it bad enough? That means that you never stop to think that anything but the best will come to you. So you are willing to put in the time and energy. Because you give it your all, you get what you want or even better. Why? Because you never stopped to think it would not happen. Optimism.

You might as well stay optimistic; anything else is too depressing.

LESSON #4 Take a Load Off:

While trying to keep busy, a common situation occurs. We stress because we feel we can not miss one opportunity to get out! You can't do everything. This leads to exhaustion. Yet, when we decide to stay home, we worry. Instead of relaxing, we just know that we are missing the only chance to meet Mr. Right. Not true! If it is the right time, the universe will make sure you show up. Don't be counterproductive; select a few great events to attend. When you stay home, make it a replenishing time. Find the best method to turn off the worried mind. I would watch the movie *"When Harry Met Sally"* over and over.

Dumb + innocent mistakes = Abundant opportunities

One of the hallmarks of readiness to meet your mate is when the idea of making a mistake is thrown out the window. This is not the time to be a perfectionist. Yes, get the outfit that looks great and you feel great in it. Yes, have your hair and makeup on right, but after this, **keep your mind on the opportunities and not on your self.** Put your sensitive little ego away for the night and get out there. There are no awards for being perfect. In fact, I am willing to say that the more mistakes you make, the more rapidly a good situation will materialize. Look at the past and realize that you always learn from the awful. So get out there and be a fool - who knows where the road may take you? Only a fool can say.

When you see a vital, interested and enthusiastic person, no matter what their age, they emanate a child's wonder at the world. Getting out and looking around can recharge that aspect of our soul.

Start creating serendipity in your life by getting out there. By finding a new person, place or thing each day, you are adding space for new opportunities to come your way. Instead of looking for exactly what you think you want, you may end up with even more than you ever dreamed of.

Getting out means you are getting closer to getting there.

As you get out "there," you will be learning about what you like and what you need. You are also enjoying this time "with yourself." This is the way to start thinking about what makes you happy and what you find interesting. You should be ready to change the pace. The next chapter will guide you through the process.

Chapter Six

CHANGING THE PACE

"Life is something you do when you can't get to sleep."
Fran Lebowitz

The time spent in Part One, "On Your Mark," was dedicated to getting the mind ready for battle. Your mental muscles were stretched. In this second section, "Get Set," the focus is on OPENING UP and LOOKING AROUND. It is time to work on the physical. This chapter forces you to start venturing out into the world. It enables you, with structured questions and activities, to gain confidence.

Cleaning up your act and taking it on the road.

There is a common wisdom that says "Clean up, throw out and make way for the new." You need to engage in activities that show the universe "I am making space for new people, places and things!" This is an opportunity to encourage the magic to begin. It clears the senses of old memories and thoughts. It creates the space for new experiences.

Cleaning, sorting, tossing and organizing, opens up much-needed space for the house and more importantly for the soul.

When you create space in your physical life, you are actually making a commitment to your goal. You are saying, "I have the space in my life for somebody new to fit it". So let's make room for him now.

HEARTWORK: MAKING ROOM PHYSICALLY.

❑ What areas of your home need to be thinned out and better organized?
❑ What items should be given away and enjoyed by somebody else?
❑ What eyesores need some paint and decorating?

❑ What things do you have in your house that are constant memories of something you would rather forget?
❑ Should you do it yourself or enlist help?
❑ Is it time to set the date for a tag sale? If so, when?
❑ Write down the names of any service you need. (e.g., rummage pickup, a closet organizer, consignment shop, painter, carpenter, decorator).

Break these tasks down into manageable segments. Create a SPRING CLEANING TASK FORCE. Assign dates to each task. Call everyone who will help. Do one hour of cleaning and sorting every day. Give yourself breaks.

After this is done, you should feel invigorated and a little bit less encumbered. Were you surprised at the number of things that you didn't need, use or even remember having? Are the cupboards clean and organized?

Get rid of old relationship memories. *When I cleared out my Christmas things, I found some old family pieces that belonged to my ex-husband. I packed these up along with some ornaments that I knew he liked (and now I loathed). I put them in a box and one morning had a friend drop them off on his front porch.*

Lose the sad and non-energizing memories.

If somebody were to move into your life, is there now room for that person? Are there extra drawers and closet space? Do you have your favorite romantic CD's, a great coffee maker, inviting sheets and candles? Could you create a wonderful meal for two at the last minute?

Once your house is in order, you have no excuse to stop you from going out to play.

MAKEOVER TIME

Now that your home is in tiptop shape, what about you? What wardrobe, makeup, accessories need to be upgraded? Why not a new look? Go ahead, it's O.K. to change. Why not check out the makeup counter for an updated lip color? What shape is your lingerie in? Are your favorite flannel pj's looking a little scary? Do you have a great robe that is in your best color? Do you love your hair?

HEARTWORK: MAKEOVER TIME

You will be dating, and your future mate will be arriving soon...are you ready?

Prioritize "makeover" items and list them from the most urgent to the least. Create a time frame to accomplish each one. If money is scarce, there are ways to get them free or on sale. I was able to win a free set of wonderful sheets and even found a beautiful robe for $15.00.

My makeover list is
Completed by this date:

1.
2.
3.
4.
5.

Are you getting excited yet?

Pulling your head out of the sand

One of the reasons to clean up the house is to feel unencumbered and excited to get out. Now is the time to explore the world of fun. "Fun" can be a serious intellectual exercise to a volleyball match on the beach. A hobby or a sports activity allows the mind to break from all the issues and worries that are occupying the brain cells. Have you been so absorbed while working with wet clay on a pottery wheel that you forget about the time, space and even the planet? As adults, we have to work at having fun.

Secret wishes

Have you been secretly wishing to DO, JOIN, PARTICIPATE IN, or TRY OUT something? Find time to try something new. Now is the time to go for it. It can be as simple as finding a wonderful new place to take a walk. I found a beach that refreshed my soul each and every time. Later, this beach was the place where my husband proposed to me. Today when I need a pick-me-up, I take a mental trip and hear the gulls, smell the sea and see the bend in the bay.

Once one simple "new" activity is developed, it is time to explore others. What hobbies have you wanted to try, or have loved but have put aside? What intellectual pursuits have you secretly longed for but don't feel justified in pursuing? Is there a whole new career that you wish you could check out? You will be writing these out below.

On the more physical realm, are you needing to stretch your muscles? Try a new sport? Check out a new piece of equipment? Are you yearning to take a class on rock climbing or wind surfing? Would a new pair of running shoes get you out and around the track? Now is the time to go for these things.

Are we working so hard at living that we have forgotten how to celebrate life?

Does your mind need a vacation? Would you like to send it to Club Med while you stay at the office and get some work done? Then you need to find the time to give your brain a rest. This will save your sanity by letting the brain focus on something other than yourself and be allowed to drift. Why? **Re-energizing occurs**.

Even a short walk in the woods can aid in this self-renewal process. Force the mind to tune in on the trees, the sounds and smells. It is similar to meditation because you are able to transport your mind to another place. This mental self-renewal will give you back much more that you expend. This enables your mind to quiet the chatter. When the mental space is cleared, new information is able to seep in.

Treat your mind to a vacation. Find something where you become lost in the process.

HEARTWORK: GET YOURSELF OUT OF THAT NICE CLEAN HOUSE, GIRL!

What can you do that really would be fun? **Listen to your heart until you hear a "zing"!**

Sarah was a sophisticated graphic designer. Most of her friends were into jazz and alternative sounds. They all abhorred Country/Western music. Yet, she had a crazy yearning to learn how to Western dance. Through friends of friends, she met a group of like-minded people. Each Thursday, they would meet and dance. As the group met in different lounges, their circle widened. They never waited long to get out onto the dance floor. Sarah danced so much that she went down two dress sizes from all the activity. She loved it! It was fun to feel the freedom of getting out on her own, meeting up with the group, staying out until 10 and still being productive the next day. It took months to learn the many styles of dance. It was addicting, fun and a fabulous way to exercise. She stopped focusing on meeting just one man and met many. Then one night a handsome man asked her to dance and thus began a wonderful new romance.

HEARTWORK: LIST THE "THINGS" THAT MAKE YOUR HEART SING.

Now let's get really clear about activities and the action plan that goes with them. Take out a pen and paper.

A List at least five activities that you want to check out. Next to each one, list when they can be done. For example, if you want to learn to ski, the season needs to be listed. Or if you want to join a book club, what times are you available?
B. After each one, write down where these can be done. Get your hands on the literature, brochures, and newsletters, and make the phone calls.
C. Place a number by each item to prioritize, from the most important to the least.
D. Can you do one of these activities in the next two weeks?
E. If it is a seasonal activity, can you get the information to get organized and plan ahead for the time of this pursuit? Make reservations and set up the time in advance.
F. How are you going to pay for this? How are you going to manage the time? How far in advance can you plan? How long of a commitment can you make? You may be able to commit to a weekend seminar and not a whole quarter of school.

> **Note**: Find activities that have little to do with your work, business or career. Try something out of your comfort zone and really shake things up!

My list went like this:

5) Walkathon	Spring
1) Class history of furniture	Quarterly
3) Lecture by writer that I admire	Look at bookstores' authors lecture schedule
1) Western Dancing	Find a friend, and where to take classes
4) Spend holidays away from city	Dude ranch for Thanksgiving (call Tucson) Ocean for Xmas (call B& B's) Cross-Canada train trip call Amtrak)
2) Auto Cad	Every other quarter

After making the phone calls and reading the brochures, I felt like I was in control of the fun in my life. I lined up friends or went by myself. I realize now that I started the trek into the next career phase of my life and had some irreplaceable adventures along the way. Did I meet people? Yes. Did I meet men? Yes! It got me in touch with all those individuals who had the time and energy to do more than just go to work and go home. It helps to know that there are so many other singles out there who are struggling to learn new things and re-learning how to have a good time.

A life full of vitality includes friends of all ages.

Meanwhile, you need relationships with men and women of all ages. In order to stay young, hang out with young people. Break out of your limited perspective of just your peers. Spend time with your pals of the opposite sex. Gain a little insight on the viewpoints of those that do not share your same chromosomes. Let them engage you in some new activities. Once you do have your perfect relationship, spare time can seem to evaporate. Add a new dimension, excitement and sparkle to your life. New experiences give you joy, make your soul smile and give you other humans to relate to. **Have a fling with the "new."**

These activities create a memorable life. Now there are new reasons to get going, other than going to work, spending the money on basics and going back to work again. Don't you often feel that life is 95% errands with only 5% left for fun, wonderment, heartfelt, and memorable moments? That sparkle comes when you have given yourself the treat of trying something new!

I have a friend who is so busy that he rarely gets a full night's sleep. Every few weeks, he crashes and sleeps for the whole day. He will work a long day in his profession, play at night in a band. On the weekends, he plays volleyball and enjoys attending sports events. He also travels to lecture and teach. In one week, he accomplishes more and has more fun than most of us do in a many months. His motto is, *"I don't want to miss out on all the fun; I'll sleep when I'm 80!"*

Children can consume a large portion of a woman's free time. It definitely makes dating a much more complicated matter. Time management is even more crucial. Remember, you don't have to go to every event where you could meet someone. **Pick a few choice activities each month.**

Teamwork and using a barter system will help in getting you some free time. Some men will pay for your baby-sitter when asking you out. There are no hard and fast rules on how to manage a life outside of the demands of motherhood. If anybody can do something well and creatively, a mother can figure this out.

Olivia is a real estate agent. Every day, she juggles her family, which includes two children. At any given time, this can include school activities, hobbies and the remodel of her home. Meanwhile, she is listing and selling homes, many involving complicated issues. She made a comment about her savvy employer. He had commented that if something needed to be done with the maximum use of time, money and energy - the working mom was the true efficiency expert!

Use your mothering expertise to win the dating game!

Now you have started the ball rolling! You are having some fun meeting some new people and learning. You are even finding the "space" to fit a new person into your busy life. It is time to move on to another aspect of "Get Set," that of organizing your sources for outside help.

Active Memories

One of my dating coach clients made a comment about a small jar of colored sand that she had in her bathroom. It had been a gift from an old boyfriend. When I asked her why she kept it out, she replied "It reminds me of him." That opened up the fact that she had not really dated in the two years since they had parted. She was shocked to realize that she had been comparing every man since, to him. Yet he had not contacted her since the move. It was time for releasing. The memory had a hold of her and it was hindering her progress. If an item reminds you of a person that you need to forget, release the person by removing the item.

If you can't bear to give it away, than wrap it up and put in storage for now.

Chapter Seven

OUTSIDE HELP

"Spirit is an invisible force made visible in all life."
Maya Angelou

Here's the good news! You don't have to do everything yourself! In every other chapter, you will be working on material that involves physical and psychological strategies. "OUTSIDE HELP" is about putting your feet up and getting help from your spiritual resources. Yet, for today's do-it-now woman, this can be a little distressing. It's O.K. to let the work get done by other sources.

It is not up to us to make it happen; it is up to us to make it clear about what we want!

I. FREE-FALLING

Have you ever heard anybody talk about giving something up and then being surprised when the very thing they wanted appeared? Have you ever wanted something so badly and not gotten it? At least not right away? When you finally did get it, wasn't it so much more wonderful than you had originally hoped for? There are two sides to the Free Falling Coin. Yes, you do need to ask for what you want. Then you need to let it go and just let life take its course.

Sometimes you need to give up the controls! Being "out of control" during the dating process can be good. In other words, we live in the world that we have preconceived. We set up specific expectations in our minds, line up our options and go for it. We get disappointed because "logically" we can't visualize the way it will happen. The missing ingredient is being open to anything that comes our way. Only through new experiences, a change in direction and walking in new terrain, can real surprises occur. This is the FREE FALL stage. By letting go, a whole arena of possibilities opens up.

Amanda had her life just so. After 15 years of teaching, her life went along smoothly. She had her classroom, her students, her family and friends. She wanted to be married but had let that thought slide. There just was not enough time and she could not foresee how that would ever change. Then everything came to a dead stop. Her wonderful father was rushed to the hospital. His time on earth seemed to be almost at an end. Amanda quickly turned everything over to a substitute and rushed to be by his side. Now, time seemed to stand still. She spent all day, every day by his side. Her only break was to go outside for a cigarette. During these breaks, she became acquainted with a man whose mother was in the next room. His name was John. Each day they talked often and would slip downstairs for a quick meal. John was not the kind of man she had originally thought of as her "type." Yet they never ran out of things to talk and laugh about. Her father passed on. John and Amanda started dating and soon were inseparable. It was her father's final wish that she find the love of her life. Now 24 years later, things are still great between them.

This story is an example of how, once we get out of our own way, **life has a chance to sneak up and surprise us.** Our mind is limiting because it "knows" what it has already experienced.

When you give up...you get it. When you forget about it...it comes to you.

POP QUIZ: The mind is a terrible thing to waste. Keeping in mind that letting go is actually a method of attraction, can you think of an example from your life when you searched for something and gave up looking? Then when you were least expecting it, there it was! Was it better than you had originally hoped for?

Stephanie just had to have <u>*the*</u> *perfect 20-year reunion outfit. She spent hours shopping in all the right places for it, yet came home empty-handed. Then, while running an errand for work in a new part of town, she saw it. It was in a small boutique that she had never heard of before. It fit perfectly. She bought it and smiled all the way back to the office.*

My story goes like this:

While I contemplated going back to college for a master's degree in Media for School Libraries, a friend got me an interview at an adversiting agency. "What the hey!" While the media job was not the right fit, the gentleman interviewing me had a brainstorm. He offered me the production manager position. He sensed that my library background was the perfect fit for this job and he was right. This launched my career in advertising, which led to the field of paper and a decade of work in the wonderful, interesting, engaging world of design and printing.

The moral to my story goes something like this: Things happen for the better when we loosen up and try some crazy new things. There is magic out there to be captured.

When you stop grasping at the now...the new arrives.

II. ANGELS, GUIDES AND OTHER DIMENSIONS

There is a reason that there are so many angel books out there. We all have angels that watch over us. It isn't just a phenomenon for television plots. Have you checked in with yours lately? It is time to apprise them of your new goal, that of finding the love of your life. It may be time to thank them for helping you out of your last peril. Do you ever feel that a dead relative or friend may be "up there" ready to help?

HEARTWORK: CHECKING IN WITH YOUR ANGEL

Write out the details of the last time you were aided by an angel. If you do not have a special story, use a friend's story that gave you that sense of recognition.

____

____

____

____

HEARTWORK: FINDING OUT ABOUT ANGELS

Research the topic of angels. Read at least one book about angels and find a story that gives you that shiver of recognition. Write down below what you found so reassuring about this.

Remember, that shiver of recognition is telling you that although your intellect may be saying "Nay-nay," there is truth to the tale. Many "feel" the truth when the hairs on their arms stand up and there is a chill down their spine. How do you experience that shiver of recognition?

____

____

The person who accomplishes the most is the first to admit that they did not do it all by themselves.

I heard from my angel during the days of deep depression when my first husband and I were separated. My self-pity was hovering around the 100 percent mark when the phone rang. He called to tell me that he had just totaled out my car. He had been on his way to a ski trip and had been hit by a semi truck. As the story unraveled, a mysterious witness was able to point the finger of blame on the truck driver. After my probing about the "witness," he admitted that she was his passenger and date. When I hung up the phone, I cried for hours. Finally, later that evening I heard a loud, clear voice in my ear. It said, "Everything is going to be all right!" I got the chills, yet knew that this voice was guiding me out of my depression and on to better times. I knew then that I would survive the divorce and that my world would someday be better.

III. MEDITATION AND PRAYER

When my second marriage was announced, I was not surprised to find that so many of my friends had been praying for me. I too had prayed and meditated to establish hope and to focus on my goal. Prayer is a powerful tool. Through prayer, you will keep positive. It is like sending a Thank You note in advance. You must put everything in the positive and proactive tense. Instead of asking, "When will my perfect mate be here?" Say, "My perfect mate is here and I am ready to meet him," or "Thank you for hearing my prayers, I will meet him when the time is right."

HEARTWORK: YOUR MANTRA

Create a short sentence or two that will be your "pull it out of the hat" prayer. It will be there when you are feeling your hope slipping. Write it down on the page and transfer it to paper. Keep it handy. Instead of wallowing in your worries, read this and try to move on.

____

____

____

The mantra/prayer that I used went like this:

> **"Dear Father, Mother, God,**
> **I know that my perfect mate is here. He is getting ready to meet me. I will know him when I see him, and I am ready. It is in your hands and in divine timing. You are all-knowing. Thank you. AMEN."**

Prayer is a verbal confirmation that your wish will be granted - it is only a matter of time.

IV. MIRACLES

When you find a need for some high-octane inspiration, check into your miracle diary. Starting today, begin collecting stories that have wonderful "otherworldly" elements of surprise in the way of help. The miracles of today are not as bold as those we have heard about from ancient times. We are much too savvy for the special effects. Today's phenomena involve quiet, small events that change our thinking and then the direction of our path.

HEARTWORK: MIRACLE DIARY

Use a separate notebook to document stories of EVERYDAY MIRACLES to use in times of doubt. They can be very minuscule or sublime. Write out four miracles from your past and add one each week from now on.

Remember that miracles are events that defy our concept of "normal" behavior. These extraordinary marvels are divinely created to get our attention and to teach us something. It can be as simple as thinking about calling a friend and having the phone ring and it is just that person. *I remember looking everywhere in the house for a key. I thought I had covered all the usual places. Finally, I gave up and took a long bath. When the phone rang, I jumped up and threw on my husband's robe. There inside the pocket was the key!*

Miracles can test or strengthen our faith. While looking for our mate, they can get us back on track or instruct us about some element that we have overlooked. Look for them and, most importantly, acknowledge them!

Here are a few miracle stories that can be your first inspirations:

Julie was feeling extremely sad. It was the beginning of the holidays, and the fact that she had no family or even any event to go to had her in a tailspin. As she sat in her office looking out onto the street, she noticed that the wind had really picked up. This stormy weather only added to her feeling of despair. Finally, she put her head down and prayed. She needed to confirm that life could be better. Right then there was a bump against her office window. An advertising sign had fallen off the building from across the street. Part of it had ripped away but the first word she saw was HOPE. It was from a Bob Hope Benefit sign but the word HOPE was all she needed to see.

***

Alice had made a breakthrough. After working for months with a counselor, she had dealt with some childhood abuse issues that she had suffered and suppressed. This progress was positive but left her drained. It was three days before Christmas and she had not done one thing. It had taken all her strength to get downtown to shop. She had gotten a few things and was ready to go home. As she headed for the door, a man passed her. He was wearing jeans and a flannel shirt. He looked her straight in the eyes. In that second, she was overwhelmed with an intense sense of powerful love. She quickly looked around for him, but he had vanished in thin air. As she stood there, she experienced feelings of hope, goodwill and a sure knowing that her future would be filled with great good things. Not all angels have wings.

Those "milagros" are simply postcards from heaven.

V. LAST-DITCH EFFORTS

When all else fails and you have done everything humanly possible, turn it over. When we let go of any single focus, we gain an opportunity to see other aspects of the bigger picture.

Look up at the sky and say, "I'm turning it over."

HEARTWORK: THOSE THREE LITTLE WORDS

You are entitled to take a break. This does not mean that you give up or are throwing aside your goal of finding your perfect mate. Think of it as a **GET OUT OF JAIL FREE CARD** (like in Monopoly). It means that you have run out of ideas and you would like somebody to take over the wheel. Go ahead and take a break! Just say, "I am turning it over!"

Fill in the blanks.

Cut this out and keep in your wallet. Remember, you can take a break!

Whenever you need to, pull out the card and really take a specific time-out. Leave it in your date book and assign yourself an ending date. Then re-enter the race.

TURN IT OVER CARD

This card entitles (name)______________________________
to **TAKE A BREAK.**

This card may be used as many times as it takes to reach the goal of finding the love of my life.

So, outside of ourselves, there are larger forces that can assist us in our search. When in despair, look back on this chapter. Remember to focus on the small things. We can be so obsessed with the "big thing" that we don't see the many other things that are happening while we are searching.

After a particularly grueling date, I called my oldest friend. She was a mother of two young children, a struggling artist, and she led a very busy life. I was complaining about yet another date that had not produced the love of my life. As my litany of woes ended, she reminded me of all that I had to be thankful for. After all, I had been to a new gourmet restaurant on a balmy spring night. She had scraped spaghetti off the wall from her 3-year-old.

I was missing the small wonders, the learning, the fun. Be thankful for the small miracles along the way. Stand back and enjoy the process by not just looking for the results! I'd forgotten about how filled with anticipation I had been, how I had rushed home, the tension of what to wear and guessing where we would go. My date actually had been very interesting, the restaurant decor innovative, and the food superb. The evening had been splendid. Just because I wasn't interested in marrying the guy, I could still celebrate what a great life I was having. Why had I spoiled my adventure by not paying attention to the small events along the way!

Take stock of the miracles scattered along the path.

Now that you have a stockpile of outside help, let's focus on some issues that can hinder us during the hunt. Chapter 8 helps you get a grip on the area of timing while you search for the love of your life.

Chapter Eight

TIMING

"Time was away and somewhere else."
Louis MacNeice 1907-63 *Meeting Point* 1935

This book is based on the assumption that all the best things in life are really surprises.

As life glides along, we are amazed at the "little incidents" that impact our lives in big ways. It is the chance encounter, overhearing a word that cracks the case, or that awkward, even stupid moment that can change everything. In finding our mate, the world will open up in mysterious ways, but not until all the elements are just right. The problem is that we are often seemingly ready, yet the universe is not.

It's hard to embrace the notion of "timing" in getting our needs met. Before we reach our goal, it seems like it will never be; yet once it's here, it seems like it was just a matter of time.

How to deal with the "when."

It is essential to "get a grip" on the timing issue. If you don't, the time spent waiting for your perfect mate will become unbearable. Learning to appreciate this time is what you will discover in this chapter. Included are specific techniques to beat the "waiting blues." By the chapter's end, you will endorse the notion of DIVINE TIMING.

We can't control the timing of events!

This is like looking for the perfect house and not finding it - only to give up and several months later, while driving to visit a friend in a neighborhood you would not normally frequent, you see the perfect house. Later, you find out that just that evening, the For Sale sign had been added to the front yard. The point is that we can't control the timing.

We can not control the WHEN!

So what can you do as you get ready to meet your perfect mate? This chapter deals with how timing is really on our side as we search for our perfect mate. I have included an exercise to create your own timing affirmations. This will shed light on the many false assumptions about controlling time. Let's take a look at how timing has worked in our lives so far.

Waiting isn't really just hanging around; you are learning about what you really want.

Couples in happy unions consistently state similar facts. When they met, they knew it was "the one" very quickly. This "knowingness" was based on an accumulation of information. This information was gathered over time. When they reviewed the first encounter, they admitted it was often not "when they had hoped." Yet in hindsight, they had gained valuable information while they waited for this event. So the time spent waiting was invaluable.

In order to know him when you see him, you need time to gather information.

When I purchased my house, I learned the fundamentals for the search. First, I made a commitment to making this process my number-one priority. This meant being flexible enough to set aside some activities so I could rush out to look at a new listing. I drew up a list of every little thing I wanted. With the Realtor, we identified my preferred neighborhoods. It was fun at first, but I became frustrated as house after house did not meet my needs. I was ready, but the housing market was not participating. I could not compromise. At one point, after six months of looking, I took a break. Then I jumped back into the search. Finally, I heard about a house that was ready for the market. I had decided that this was the last house that I would look at. The house was a dream! Yet, because I was so weary from the hunt, I did not realize what a great place this was. Then the Realtor made me pull out my list. Sure enough, my "house to be" had all of the elements on the list save one. It also had many other assets that I had not dared to add to the initial list. When I made the offer, I felt a total sense of calm. I knew that if it was right it would easily be mine.

Fundamentals for the SEARCH

- ❑ We may be ready, but the object of our search may not be available...yet.
- ❑ Even when it seems right, double-check the "list."
- ❑ Others may guide us to new information, so trust and enlist the aid of others.
- ❑ It is O.K. to take a short break, but get back in there fighting.

- ❑ Keep looking and never compromise! I looked at 94 houses, and probably as many men.
- ❑ Even though it is disappointing to not find what you want, each preview is giving you more and more information.
- ❑ You might not recognize it at first glance, so don't be deceived by the first sighting.
- ❑ You will have total confidence and a sense of peace when it is right.

There is a reason for the process of hunting!

This correlation of hunting for a house and looking for a mate helps us see the pattern. So many obvious steps are similar in both pursuits:

1. Committing to the hunt
2. Creating the list, defining the qualities, updating as more information comes in, putting everything possible on the list aiming for 80% of your wants
3. Being willing to set the time aside
4. Prioritizing activities to make this a number-one goal
5. Coming face to face with illusions
6. Staying alert
7. Being eternally optimistic
8. Gaining perspective by looking at the project from different angles and perspectives
9. Taking time out when weary
10. Getting back in the game
11. Knowing it when you see it
12. Knowing that when it is right, it will work out.

As we gather information for the list, we change our opinions about what is best for us. For example, we may think a man should be at least five years older. This perception can be altered when we meet a younger man who seems so interesting and appealing. Much like the house hunter who is determined to find the old-world charm and ends up in a new condo. After much searching, he discovered that in reality, he had no extra time and little money for costly renovations. He's now found at home on Saturday, happily reading books on old houses and not on a ladder scraping paint.

DIVINE TIMING guarantees "on-time" delivery every time. In the realm of the universe and ethereal laws, there is a law of timing.

This law, called "Divine Timing," states that an event only takes place when it is the absolute perfect moment. How do we know that this applies to everyone who is seeking their perfect mate? By asking those who have successfully achieved just this goal.

Everyone that I have interviewed has stated that "when all was said and done, the timing could not have been more perfect."

With experience comes clarification.

Another issue is that of looking so much that a pattern of disappointment is created. You can look so much, and when you don't find what you want, become perpetually gloomy. It is hard to keep up your faith as date after date seems to not pan out. You may need an occasional break from all this hunting. This is fine. You know what revives you. These times are designed to give your emotions and energy a time of renewal.

HEARTWORK HINDSIGHT AND TIMING

Take a quick look back at an event in your life when you got something that you really wanted. Try to find an event or acquisition that came later than you had originally planned. How did time play an important role in helping you better define what you wanted? Did you then know it when you saw it? Was it a great surprise when it was accomplished? An example of this might be a new car or college degree. How can these steps to getting what you wanted in the past help you wrestle with the issue of waiting for your perfect partner?

Why are you so certain that this IS the right time for you? In seeking the perfect mate, many women have a preconceived notion that this is the time. Chances are, peer pressure or outside influences may increase your sense of urgency to accomplish this task. How many times over this lifetime do we need to hear our parents questioning us with, "Just because those others are doing it, why must you do it too?" It is still correct to want "it," but be clear about why. If you understand that this pressure is making the hunt seem endless, you must let it go, knowing that it will come when it is right for you.

Stacy felt stressed. She had gone to so many wedding and baby showers that she could just about gag, when yet another invitation arrived in the mail. It seemed just too depressing that all her pals were creating their families and buying new homes, while she was still in her apartment, looking for a roommate to help with the rent. She was not even dating anybody in particular. She felt her time had just about run out. Yet she could not give up on her dream of a great marriage with two wonderful children. She found a new roommate. Several weeks after moving in, her roommate asked Stacy if she would be interested in meeting a man from her work. Stacy said "Sure," without much hope that this would be any great event. Stacy met John and their first date was pretty good. On the next date, she really started to like him, and by the fourth date, she knew he was "the one." They had so much in common, love of great food (she was a gourmet cook and he was a food exporter/importer), love of family, travel, language and more. They were married one year later. All her wishes came true, as she gave birth to her first child at age 38 and the next at 41.

Her only regret? Not having the faith that good things were coming IN THEIR OWN TIME.

***

Claire was resolved at 49 that she would stop fretting about not being married. Along with this new attitude, she had adopted the "just go for it" approach to life. If something fun came up, enjoy! So on Friday night when the work gang decided to go out for drinks, she went along. One of the women had invited a friend from out of town to join them. Claire ended up in his car helping him with the directions to find the restaurant. He was surprised that she knew so much about his line of work. Later, they decided to meet for a date, and the next time that he came to town, he looked her up. Claire kept her new attitude until about the fourth date, when they both realized how much they had in common and what a great time they always had together. On Valentine's Day he presented her with an engagement present, a brand new bright red Jaguar convertible. They are now married and still having a wonderful time. It was definitely worth the wait.

What she learned? We must give up the reins on WHEN it is right, and enjoy each moment.

TIMING (Athletics & Sports): ***"The regulating of the speed of a motion, stroke, blow, etc., so as to cause it to reach its maximum at the correct moment."***

(Webster's New Collegiate Dictionary)

Taming the Heebie-Jeebies

Often our frustrations can become overwhelming. The waiting can seem endless. This feeling of helplessness in being unable to create the "timing" is often excruciating. Usually, we are by ourselves and caught in an endless "I never get what I want!" self-pity session. I call this the Heebie-Jeebies. You know the scene: It is 3:00 a.m. and you have just realized that you are going to be an 80-year-old bag lady with three cats following you through the streets. It gets worse, as you see yourself dip behind a dumpster to tidy up for just one more "Blind Date." It is then that you know you have ruined your life by not marrying that nerd in Chemistry class.

Block it out by shouting back! You must eliminate these fears about timing: "It will never happen. I can't keep waiting. It is too late. It is not for me. I have missed it." And so on. These fears can be countered by the YELLOW BELLY SCREAM AND HOLLER PHRASE BOOK!

These phrases are scientifically programmed to de-stigmatize negative mental images caused by having to wait for your perfect mate to appear on the scene. It is advisable to yell these affirmations out loud:

1. "I know what I want in a husband. It's the job of my guides, angels, the Universe and God to bring him to me. They must have a really great reason for this apparent delay."

2. "The only thing I have to be is alert."

3. "There is an infinite number of ways to meet my perfect mate. It will only take a second to recognize him and only a second for my whole life to change."

4. "There is no way that he has slipped by me. The Universe will make sure that I get as many chances as it takes to meet him."

5. "I can not control the timing in my life. Everyone has their own unique timing of events."

6. "My perfect mate is coming and I am ready."

7. "I am turning this project over to the Universe, and therefore I do not need to spend any time worrying about it."

8. "I know that I deserve the best and it is coming. I will not give up."

9. "When all is said and done, the timing will seem impeccable."

HEARTWORK: CREATE YOUR OWN YELLOW BELLY SCREAM & HOLLER PHRASE BOOK

Take some time out now and create your own phrases that will help you combat the Heebie-Jeebies. Make sure that they are positive and, when possible, in the present tense. Leave these notes where you may need them in an emergency. They can be stored by the bed, in the shower and in your car. When possible, scream these out. The brain needs to be reprogrammed for the positive, and the volume seems to help. I would yell mine out each morning on the way to work. They went like this:

"My perfect mate is here."
"I will be married soon."
"I am ready to meet my perfect mate."
"He is ready to meet me."
"I will have the greatest marriage ever."
and
"I will know him when I see him!"

"The timing in my life is perfect."

There are other elements interacting with the timing.

Forcing the event to happen prematurely will only create problems.

There is an enormous importance to having an open and optimistic attitude. You need to have a respect for the TIMING OF LIFE'S EVENTS. You need to treat yourself very well. Vitality is needed as you go about your business. Often we need to review our background and all the areas of life where we have found what we wanted. Many of these were only resolved long after we thought they should have occurred. Yet in hindsight, they really seem to have happened at the precise right moment. So many people, while reviewing their lives, comment on the synchronicity and the perfect rhythm of the events of their lives. There is progress being made behind the scenes. This is the time to apply heavy doses of faith to your consciousness.

We eliminate the 'surprise' factor when we force the timing.

I just got off the phone with my dear father. His news was about his best friend of 45 years named Ned. It seems that the recently widowed Ned has just married his third wife. My Dad asked me, "I'll bet you will never guess who he married?" "No, I can't Dad." He chuckled as he replied, "His secretary!" She had been his secretary for over twenty-five years. During those years, she had divorced and raised two children while working full-time in Ned's law firm. She knew Ned better than almost anybody! Now they are both retired and traveling on exotic trips around the world. Are they surprised? Not really. Are they happy? Absolutely! Here is a great example of how timing's unpredictability is often part of the fun.

Faith is not a comparative thing: when things are going right, you believe, and when things are not going your way, you give up. It should be the opposite: when things are not going well, you know it is for a reason, and when things are going well, you give thanks in a kind of reaffirmation."

Remember that everything has a reason. There is divine timing going on all the time. Hindsight is our only friend when it comes to timing. Until then, optimism and perseverance will have to do!

In the next section, entitled *"Working from a List,"* we will develop the strongest asset in the hunt.

PART III.
GET READY... Using tools

"A man falls in love with his eyes, a women through her ears."
Woodrow Wyatt, *To The Point*, London Sunday Times, 22 Mar 81

Chapter Nine

WORKING FROM A LIST

"Love talked about can be easily turned aside, but love demonstrated is irresistible."
W. Stanley Mooneyham, *Word Books*, 1978

In this third section of the book, you will be creating tools to aid in the search for the love of your life. You will be identifying personal qualities in five homework assignments.

Clarification comes from experience and concrete methods of information-gathering.

List-making is said to be a cure for sleeplessness and scatter-brained confusion, and a way of controlling the chaos in our part of the universe. By making a list, our mind can move on to other more creative thoughts. It is used to ensure that we get what we want in the grocery store or in our future mate. The process of list-making enables us to catalog information in categories. In finding the perfect mate, it is the backbone and the lifeline to getting what you want. The more information you gather, the more confident you will become.

How does one gather up all the needed characteristics that will define a perfect mate? It seems like a mighty tall order. After all, we will need to stay enchanted with him for a lifetime! How is it done?

Very, very carefully!

Lists are used to DEFINE what we want and CONFIRM when we find it.

Of all the activities that you can do to catch Cupid, this is the most important! You must create a wish list of all the characteristics that you want in your future mate. The good news is that you can get as exacting and specific as you dare hope for. On the other hand, you can't go back later (say, after five years of marriage) and change, delete or add. Challenging, isn't it?

When a friend of mine thought about what she wanted she put, "He will have a house in Europe and a Swiss bank account." Well, the next man she met was from Switzerland and had an apartment in Geneva, and, of course, a Swiss bank account. So get creative and put everything you've ever thought you wanted on THE LIST!

Words are the building blocks for the structure of our dreams!

While you read this book, do the homework and date - you must be constantly adding to THE LIST. It will become the balance sheet, a sort of record-keeping mechanism to use as a reference when you meet your perfect mate. When you are in the romantic stage, it acts as a litmus test to weigh his assets and liabilities. The list acts as a counterpoint to our racing mind when Mr. Perfect arrives and big decisions are being made for the future. When push comes to shove, the list acts as a proving ground, when compromises arise and second-guessing kicks in. All in all, the list is the final vote to embrace a lifelong relationship OR move on to other candidates.

I am not a believer in the "opposites attract" school of relationships. The more you have in common with your mate, the better your chances of a successful relationship. Why? **The more you have in common, the less you have to compromise!** The less time you spend compromising, the more time you will have together enjoying the things you both like to do!

This is why the list-making begins with YOUR qualities, interests and attributes. They are the foundation of THE LIST. If you love to travel, adore dogs and crave old architecture, it couldn't hurt if he had those same interests. This holds true for your past. The more you two match from a historical perspective, the better your chances of creating a lasting union.

The cornerstone for a long-term relationship consists of common experiences and similar goals for the future.

The "YOU" List

Before you list those traits that best define the love of your life, ask yourself this: "What are my attributes?" Being aware of these personal qualities enables you to validate their special worthiness in the Relationship Sweepstakes. Create phrases that give you a quick boost when you are disappointed.

Some examples might be: "Well, he'll never get to munch on my killer chocolate chip cookies or dine on my Irish stew. He will never know what a great present-giver I am and how I love to host dinner parties. He'll never know that I can ski, play tennis, hike, fish, canoe, and kayak. He'll never get to visit my log cabin or ride my brother's horse. He'll never get to hear one of my seminars and spend a rainy day just reading the paper with me. He's not going to experience any of the many hugs and kisses and laughter at the end of the day. Tough luck, Mister!"

The equation goes like this:

The more you like yourself + The more you have in common The greater your chance at happiness

HEARTWORK: "I'M GREAT AND HERE'S WHY" PART ONE

Use your notebook and list all of your personal qualities. These are the things that demonstrate your uniqueness. Add qualities from your spiritual, mental, physical, psychological and intellectual sides. If you are blocked, call friends and solicit 5 qualities from each. After this, create a "personal mantra" of how great you are. This can be pulled out when you are feeling rejected or need a boost to get back into the playing field.

Here are some of the qualities that can be included:
Lovable, loving, lovely
Happy, humorous, healthy
Elegant, enchantress, enchanting
Outgoing, compassionate
Fun, funny, focused on others
Vitality, reliable, rational
Smart, witty
Well-read, responsible
Good cook, when I want to be
Good friend, good daughter, good aunt, good coworker
Good with money
Generous
Good listener
Up for anything
Interesting, interested in many topics
Like the outdoors

Part Two. Circle the attributes that you desire in your perfect mate. Add these to THE LIST.

As the weeks go by, you will find that you need to fine-tune each phrase. Make sure that you are absolutely clear about each definition. One example of fine-tuning is that you may think that you want your perfect mate to be artistic. Then you date an artist and he is too spontaneous, too messy and too broke. You will need to go back to the list and edit. The new qualities might be "generous, grounded and successful artist."

We often take for granted the meaning of a word. "Polite" to you may seem "cold" to me.

Each word or characteristic needs to be evaluated for the meaning it has to you. I had originally written "smart" on my list. After dating several men with exceedingly enormous IQ's and not having any fun, I realized that my definition was not quite exact. I wanted somebody who was intelligent. Not someone so bright that everyday matters were beyond his grasp. I wanted somebody who was well-read and articulate. When I could not understand him and he seemed to think he was superior to me, I felt miserable. I hated it when a man talked down to me. My list was revised to include "naturally intelligent," a good conversationalist and well-read, with the ability to discuss what was going on in his own head as well as a book he has read.

What kind of person makes you feel great? What qualities create this magic? Define it!

The No List

As you draw up THE LIST, there need to be at least three items that are absolutely non-negotiable. As you spend time on these do's and don'ts, what are the three main things that you will NOT stand for? It might be alcoholism, smoking, egomaniac, doesn't want to be a father and so on. These are the NON-NEGOTIABLES. They will help you narrow the field. All you need to do is create tools of perception to ferret out these qualities in the men you meet. Some of these include issues of religion, physical traits, work ethics, drugs, alcohol, family matters.

Before you get to "yes," know your "no's."

You need to define what is truly unacceptable. I started out my NO LIST with "No beards, bores or bullies." I did not want a man with a beard. My image was of a shaggy, scratchy thing attached to a lazy human being. I finally took that detail off the list. What would happen if my perfect mate had a beard and I rejected him? A beard could be shaved off. My husband has a very short tailored beard, one that I miss when he shaves it off, and one that adds to his handsome good looks. I later revised my three no's to the three "b's": "No bores, bullies or boozers." The moral of the story is that each item needs to be looked at CAREFULLY!

HEARTWORK: THE THREE NO-NO'S

In the spaces below, write out your THREE NO-NO's. These are traits that are absolutely unacceptable issues. Really do some soul-searching on these. They will be the only negatives on a list of positive traits. These are the items that you will not negotiate on. The rest of the list is a wish list of hopes.

1.
2.
3.

Later you will add the THREE NO's to the top of THE LIST. It will take some time to fine-tune these.

This is also a time to explore the notion of a type of man that you want. I just received a call from a friend who said she had decided that Jimmy Stewart was her type of guy. He demonstrated so many qualities that she wanted in her next husband. She stated that he was honest, spiritual, tall (her former husband had been short and roly-poly), funny, up-front, emotional, and so on. There began her list of qualities.

HEARTWORK: MOVIE IDOL MADNESS

Stop and think about your matinee idol. What does he look like and what do you know about his personality? What is appealing about the character that he played?

Add these to THE LIST, the really big "PERFECT MATE" List

You have started to gather information from Chapter 3, ***"CLOSING THE BARN DOOR,"*** in the section "Autopsy of Boyfriends Past." As you gather characteristics and qualities, start writing them down. Later you can have categories. You will need to fine-tune and rewrite until the time comes when you know enough is enough already. Then tuck this away and save it for the time when you meet Mr. Right. Pull it out then to double-check his qualities with those on your list. All through the book I will be referring to this as **THE LIST.**

HEARTWORK: THE MAGICAL "MY PERFECT MATE" LIST

Turn to your notebook and begin **THE LIST.**

Create the list of all the qualities for your future perfect mate. Everything must be phrased in the positive. Instead of saying, *"I don't want him to smell,"* try a phase like, *"Clean, and I will love his smell. He will wear aftershave and take lots of showers."* Later, fit all of your adjectives into specific categories.

- ✓ **SOCIAL**
- ✓ **GOALS**
- ✓ **MENTAL**
- ✓ **SPORTS**
- ✓ **PHYSICAL**
- ✓ **ATTITUDE**
- ✓ **SPIRITUAL**
- ✓ **CULTURAL**
- ✓ **EMOTIONAL**
- ✓ **PERSONALITY**
- ✓ **ABOUT MONEY**
- ✓ **INTELLECTUAL**
- ✓ **NEATNESS**
- ✓ **HOBBIES**
- ✓ **ATTITUDE**
- ✓ **BACKGROUND**
- ✓ **PROFESSIONAL**
- ✓ **PHILOSOPHICAL**
- ✓ **FUTURE**
- ✓ **ABOUT THE PAST**
- ✓ **SEXUAL**
- ✓ **ROLE AS FATHER AND HUSBAND**
- ✓ **BROTHER**
- ✓ **SON**
- ✓ **BAGGAGE WILLING TO PUT UP WITH**

Include how he feels about you, his past, his goals, his achievements, his relationship to his parents, his friends, his children, his ex-wives and his profession. What is his education, hobbies, skills, desire for travel, kind of movies and entertainment? Is he a day person or a night owl? What does he do in his spare time? What are his goals of marriage and partnership? Is he honest, trustworthy, successful? How is his money management? Is he in touch with his feelings? How much affection does he give and need?

Don't forget to explore how he deals with his friends and how they speak about him, as well as how they will deal with you. Describe his role as father, stepfather and husband.

HEARTWORK: ONE-WORD DESCRIPTION

Find one word that will exactly describe your perfect mate. Write this below and then add this to your list.

____.

The word that I used was "KIND." The word "kind" meant that he was a humanitarian, giving, benevolent, not a big ego, loving and so on. It is essential to be able to summarize your desire in such simple terms. Other one-word descriptions might be: TRUSTWORTHY, FOCUSED, COMPASSIONATE, POSITIVE, HAPPY, FUN-LOVING, PLAYFUL, NURTURING, HONEST, OUTGOING or GENEROUS.

Jessie worked in a doctor's office. For many months, a really nice man named Jeff had been coming in. Jessie was dating a few dreary men. Jeff had just completed a rather grisly divorce, yet he always had a kind word to say and an optimistic approach to the rest of his day. Each time he left, Jessie wanted to protect him from any further nastiness. Jeff would often stay and talk and laugh. Soon Jessie found herself wondering which one of her friends she should fix up this eligible bachelor with. He seemed so nice and so fun to be around. She knew he would make somebody (who really appreciated him} a very nice husband. One day, Jeff walked in and asked her out. She was surprised at first, but after the first date, she realized he was just what she had wanted...a nice, fun, caring man. They were engaged after the fourth date.

Had Jessie created THE LIST to refer to, she would have realized early on that Jeff had many of the characteristics she wanted in a mate. By referring to a LIST as a tool, she would have rapidly known that he was a prime candidate for her perfect mate.

On the other hand, there is my friend Melissa. She compiled her list and that very day she met her future partner.

Melissa was ready to get out and date. As an events planner, she knew how to use her time to its maximum potential. After her divorce, her attempts at creating a relationship had turned out poorly. She could not figure out why she was not meeting the kind of man she wanted to spend the rest of her life with. One thing was clear, she did not want anyone who even remotely resembled her first husband. He had been a high-profile, dramatic, big-wheeler, all show and no warmth kind of a guy. With this in mind, she marched into a dating service and proceeded to fill out the questionnaire. She was forced to compile a list of the attributes that she did want. Melissa spent quite a bit of time on this, and then off she went to an event that she had coordinated. As she drove there, she reviewed what she wanted in a mate. She was surprised at how she wanted a gentle, caring, affectionate man who was a good listener, among many other characteristics. When she arrived, the manager of the facility walked over to meet her. He was a tall, rather shy, nice, non-assuming gentleman. They sat and talked. Later that evening they met for coffee. He was not the type of man that she was usually was attracted to. Yet, as she reflected on THE LIST, he fit perfectly into her new mate qualifications.

THE LIST keeps you on track to getting what you really want. This clarification is essential, and the fun part is that you can add as much or as little as you wish on it.

Clarity combined with confidence creates results!

The valuable tool called THE LIST is started. You will be adding to it, while you read the book and as you meet men. To build the most comprehensive list, tune in to the following chapters. They are designed to help you focus on specific areas in the list-building process.

Chapter Ten

DEFINING LOVE

"Someone asked me to name the time our friendship stopped and love began. Oh, my darling, that's the secret. Our friendship never stopped."
Lois Wyse, *Non Stop, Love Poems for the Very Married*, 1968

Hopefully THE LIST is growing larger and longer. Have you been fine-tuning each word to make sure that the clarity is precise? Are you certain that your definition and the universal meaning of the word is understood? Before you tuck this list away, read this chapter to focus on some issues and qualities that will make your future union ironclad.

Advocacy vs. Love

"Love" is a many-splendored thing, but is so overused that the definition is somewhat muddy. Often in relationships it is unwittingly used as a two-edged sword. An example might be the battered wife who won't leave her husband because she still "loves" him. Yes, love is essential. I know that you will love this future mate and that he will feel the same. It's just that I find it hard to define love in everyday practical terms. So let's get even more specific about what love in the real world is all about.

Wade through the muddy waters of love and you will find advocacy shining at the bottom of the pond.

As a single woman, I was doing really well. I had friends and activities. I had a house and lots of interests. What did I want from a relationship that I did not have already? I remembered days in my previous marriage when I dreaded going home because of the possible conflict and disappointment that awaited my arrival. Yet, coming home to an empty house was difficult too. What was it that I could not do for myself that I needed from this man?

This is the mental picture of what I wanted. *I would come through the door and there he would be. He would give me a hug and a kiss and ask me how my day was. He would not settle for an "O.K." from me but ask me for specifics. He would listen and understand my perspective. He would ask me for my ideas and think they were great. I, too, would be a part of his working life. I would know about the kind of environment he worked in and what his long-term plans were. We would know about each other's coworkers and clients. He was on my side no matter what the issues would be. Our goals for the future would be tied together to mutually benefit each other and the relationship as a whole.*

When I found the word that summarized this kind of love, I knew that this quality would last for an entire lifetime, because it generated so much caring for each other. My perfect mate would be my advocate and ally. This is the kind of love you need from your future mate. **Your future partner needs to get a kick out of you.**

HEARTWORK: DEFINING LOVE IN TODAY'S WORLD

So with the Cole Porter song "I Get a Kick Out of You" singing in your brain, take out a pen and do the assignment below.

Look up the words "ally" and "advocacy." Describe below a typical evening with your future mate. Incorporate these qualities in the way he treats you.

Add these attributes to the list.

The best word for a partnership characteristic is ADVOCACY.

There is one aspect of love that outshines all of love's other attributes. This is the function of advocacy in a partnership. Early in the dating phase and well into the aging of the relationship, this is essential. In sickness and health, and during the day-to-day activities that constitute a relationship - advocacy is the glue that binds.

"ADVOCATE" the act of pleading for, supporting or recommending; active espousal. syn: champion, proponent, backer.

The Random House Dictionary of the English Language. Second Edition.

The interrelationship between the two parties must be based on a deep respect and love for each other. From this foundation, the relationship can grow and maintain its growth because of the stable structure that it resides on. If each individual advocates for and promotes the other, then the relationship can survive most of the forces that come against it. You can only advocate for something you respect and believe in. This accounts for the living, growing and changing aspect of the relationship. It aids in ensuring the longevity of the relationship. This allows the other person to become the most that they wish for. It allows you to live this life with peace.

Advocacy is the most indispensable aspect of love in a relationship. It is essential to have advocacy as the backbone of any long-term relationship.

Cynthia was trying to adjust to her new life. Her husband of thirty years had died of a heart attack. Since he had been a physician, there was the practice to sell and the office to staff. Cynthia lost not only her best friend and husband, but her employer as well (she had done the books for all those years). One day the phone rang and a voice from the past spoke. The caller was her old boyfriend from college named Sid. He had heard about her husband's death and did not even wait one day to phone and find out how she was. He was considerate and sympathetic. He too had lost his wife and understood the shock and confusion. He arranged for them to meet for lunch the next week. This started a short and exhilarating engagement. The minute Cynthia sat down to lunch, she found the most attentive and loving man - one who was very interested in her welfare above all else. Throughout the years, he had inquired through mutual friends about how she was. They were married several months later and are growing old together with nurturing love. The moral is that advocacy for a person rarely changes.

Here is a great example of advocacy and love. This endorsement of your partner, together with his endorsement of you, is the one factor that will ensure harmony no matter what else collides with the relationship. It creates an aura of ease when conflict arises. In its simplest form, this championing of another is simply love.

Advocacy fuels the synergy in a relationship.

When two people are charged with advocacy for one another, the scope of what can be accomplished can totally surpass the activity of one person. When energy and creativity are combined with cooperation, collaboration and teamwork, a perpetual state of synergy exists. The long-lasting effects encompass continued growth, excellent communication and inspired perceptions. This alignment creates an environment of positive growth that can last a lifetime.

Respect

Alignment occurs in direct proportion to the amount of "commonality" that exists between two people. Common goals, values and morals are essential to the advocacy process. In order to promote your partner, you need to be in agreement. All this needs to be sorted out before the pact to lifetime commitment is mutually agreed upon.

In order to experience the other's portfolio of values, likes, dislikes, morals, ethics and philosophical inclinations, you need to spend time with the other person.

Respect is another essential ingredient on both sides of a relationship. The thesaurus defines it as: *N .respect, consideration, cour-*

tesy, attention, deference, reverence, honor, esteem, estimation, veneration, admiration; approbation, etc.

V .respect, regard, revere, reverence, honor, venerate, hallow; esteem, think much of, entertain respect for, look up to, defer to, pay attention to, pay respect to, do honor to; do the honors to; hail, show courtesy, pay homage to,.command respect, inspire respect; awe, impose, overawe, dazzle.

While you evaluate your potential partner, consider his attitude towards you. Is he respectful of you, your time, your opinions, your career, your family, your children, your pets, your belongings, your beliefs, your spirit? Is he reliable, trustworthy and responsible? This is why time is needed to observe this man and how he reacts in these areas. Reserve your judgment of him while this time transpires.

Gather up a historical profile on him by observing his interplay with people from his past. What does he tell you about his family, his ex-wife, past girlfriends, friends from school, his children, and employers and employees? Is he respectful to all living things? Are there others who deeply respect him? Finding a man who is respectful and one who advocates for you can create a very safe environment for you to live and grow in.

Longevity and love are affixed by the application of advocacy.

One reason that dating and engagement time exist is to better understand the other person. Or better stated, it is a series of events to help us see how we feel. The more types of activities and interrelating, the more information can be accumulated. Keep using these as opportunities for checking how you feel. It is not just to find out how he rolls the toothpaste tube and how he likes his mother. **It is to observe how he deals with the basic ups and downs of life.**

Watch out for snippets of his past that come your way. Stay as objective as possible. This is a time when you may be in a "cloud" of endearing, overwhelming, not-in-touch-with-reality kinds of perceptions. However, it can be done.

Some of the questions that need to be answered include:

1. Job history: why has he left each position?
2. Ex-wife and ex-significant girlfriend: what are his comments about her?
3. What is his basic religious ideology?
4. What are his passions, desires and goals for the future?
5. What are his pet peeves and things that annoy him?
6. What issues arise jealousy, envy, joy, laughter?
7. Is he an empathetic person?
8. Does he validate your view of the world?

Advocacy from your partner is like winning the lottery for life. Having an unconditional lover-friend on your side for life can have some outstanding results. In the big ways and in the little ways, you need to know that he is on your side. In the most respectful manner, is he:

✓ Nurturing?
✓ Listening?
✓ Paying attention?
✓ Enjoying you?
✓ Respectful?
✓ Making time to be with you?

Check mate

These are just some of the ways to check and see if you have an advocate for a mate. **Essentially, does he like your take on life?**

A QUICK TEST for checking on advocacy.

When he calls you after you have been with him, does he follow up with questions about the issues in your life that you mentioned previously? For example, you had dinner the night before. You needed to get home early because you had a meeting that you were chairing early the following morning. When he calls the next afternoon, does he ask you how the meeting went? In other words, does he remember things that are important to you and does he check in to see how your life is going?

When you are together, how does he act towards you?

Yes, even today, the act of opening doors shows his level of respect and caring, even the level of his desire to please you. Even if he doesn't have to use these manners on a daily basis, you know that he has been taught them and wants to please you above himself.

Mind his manners.

Of all the data that you gather about this man, the most impor-

- **Does he listen to you and make a comment to create conversation?**
- **Does he promote you to his friends, coworkers and family?**
- **Does he ask about your day and remember the significant issues in your life?**
- **Does he follow up with questions relating to information gathered from your conversations?**
- **Does he share?**
- **How does he interrelate between issues you have with your family and friends?**
- **Does he greet you with enthusiasm and respect?**
- **Is he always on your side?**

tant is that of his advocacy for you. Only by experience and deep conversations are you able to best understand his morals, values, ethics and personality. How close are these to yours? Add everything you can about these issues to THE LIST.

Next, let's explore some of the myths about communication and money matters in compiling your list. Chapter 11 will open up some thought-provoking issues.

Chapter Eleven

LOOKING UNDER THE HOOD

"We can not judge either the feelings or the character of men with perfect accuracy, from their actions or their appearance in public; it is from their careless conversation, their half-finished sentences, that we hope with the greatest probability of success to discover their real character."
Maria Edgeworth 1767-1899

The analogy of "looking under the hood" is to draw attention to some of the fine-tuning needed in the search for Mr. Right. When you are looking for a used car, you most likely know which car you want just by sight. When you find one for sale, you still need to investigate how the car runs, how many miles, how you fit behind the wheel, the condition of the interior and what the price is.

So too, in creating a long-term life commitment, you need to "look under the hood" at some important issues. Number one is his conversation style. This creates YOUR COMMUNICATION STYLE as a couple. This must be top-notch. Why?

How you communicate can be more important than what you are communicating about.

So much time in a relationship is spent in COMMUNICATION. In fact, a "relationship" is 100% communication, whether it be verbal, physical and or mental. By doing couple time homework, you will be better able to define your communication style and the best companion style for you.

Talk can make or break a relationship.

What is so important about communication? **Through conversation, we get our needs met!** We hold discussions about future plans, to try to get our emotions understood, to create strategies, make changes and generally navigate all the avenues we venture into as a couple. In the car analogy, you may have found the perfect car, but if the engine is too noisy or it is a gas hog, you need to keep moving for another car. It is too costly or perhaps impossible to fix this. So you may "love" this man but if you can't get him to communicate...keep looking. When I say "looking," I mean look more than at the outside appearance. Listen and look past the exterior condition. It is essential to have excellent communication with each other.

At one point, I had a boyfriend that fit the bill in many ways. We had been dating for many months when I needed to talk about some emotional "stuff." He could not deal with it. He was an engineer and could fix absolutely anything, but when it came to dealing with his or my emotions, he became frozen. I cried for hours and the next day I knew that I was a very verbal person and it was essential for me to be with somebody I could "talk" to especially about things from the heart and soul.

Components of Communication

Let's face it, we live in a very visual world. We are blinded by what we see before we get to what we "hear." Our first impulse is to focus on our first impression - his looks. We might buy a sofa because it "looks" perfect to us. Sight is our first clue about a person. Yet once we meet someone and spend time with them, the visual takes a back seat to all the elements of sound. WHAT is being said and HOW it is being expressed are building blocks for communication.

Have you noticed that the happiest couples seem to have great lines of communication? One of the reasons that they express themselves well is that each partner respects the other's opinion. They may not be in total agreement but they have a style that works!

It was love at first sound.

Get clear about how communication occurs between the two of you. It is never too early to start finding your comfort area of conversation. Start using these on the first date. Right from the beginning, by listening between the lines, you can learn about his attitude about you and his plans for a long-term commitment.

The four COMMUNICATION COMPONENTS are:

1. HOW he talks to you:
   - ❑ Does he engage you in the conversation?
   - ❑ Is he too analytical, technical, vague or dull?
   - ❑ Is his pace comfortable?
   - ❑ Is he listening to you?
   - ❑ Is he respectful of you?
2. WHEN he talks to you:
   - ❑ Does he lecture or dialog, never letting you in?

- ❑ Is there an easy ebb and flow?
- ❑ Can you get a word in?
- ❑ Is he looking at you?

3. WHAT he talks about:
   - ❑ Are they topics of interest?
   - ❑ Are these original thoughts or just pickup lines?
   - ❑ Is he articulate?
   - ❑ Is he evasive?
   - ❑ Do you like his "take" on things?
   - ❑ Do you share similar interests and goals?
   - ❑ Can you tell that he is genuinely interested in you by his conversation?
4. WHY he talks to you.
   - ❑ Does he engage you in his decision-making? Do you act as a sounding board?
   - ❑ Does he let you know what he is stressed about?
   - ❑ Does he check in with you during the day, just to hear how you are?
   - ❑ Is his conversation peppered with optimistic com - ments about the world?
   - ❑ Does he let you know how much he values you and the relationship
5. DOES he make you laugh?

When is the time to start identifying his conversation style? How do you do this? By starting a conversation **right from the beginning!** Then you need to not only listen to his reply, you need to keep the conversation going. As in a volleyball game, you need to be a great server as well as keeping the volley going.

An example might be: *"Wow, I really like your briefcase! Where did you find it? You must have bought it outside of the country — or is it an old family heirloom?"* This gives him a chance to fill in where he found the briefcase and a little history. It is positive and it sounds original and open-ended.

HEARTWORK: TONGUE-WAGGING LINES PART ONE:

Who are the people that you communicate with very well? Why are your conversations with them so exceptional? Define the conversational style. ______________________________

An example is "witty and a punster," a person who can make verbal word puns while he talks.

While meeting and dating men, you must develop and practice methods to get a conversation started. How else are you going to gather data on how he feels about life? Practice ways to get men to talk. A statement like "Wow, now tell me — did your mother pick out that tie?" can actually get the tongues a-wagging.

PART TWO: Take out a pen and write out three lines that might work with a perfect stranger to get him engaged in conversation.

If you are stuck on this assignment, call a man friend and ask him what he would like to hear or be asked. Then memorize and have on hand to use at any moment!

____

____

____

Conversation can be the most soothing of pleasures.

Conversation is food for my soul. From the first date forward, quality events are measured by the words flowing to create verbal excitement. I love to listen as new ideas come forth and get bandied about. My most memorable dinner parties consist of several intense debates around the table. Who cares about the food, wine and decor...listen to the words flying! My dessert is sitting back later and replaying the great verbal moments.

HEARTWORK: WHAT ARE YOUR FAVORITE CONVERSATION TOPICS?

Add common conversation topics to the list. List them by using this sentence. "He will share my interest in ________________.

Examples might be:

❑Politics ❑News ❑Sports ❑History ❑Metaphysics ❑Travel

Find out if he has similar interests by getting them into YOUR CONVERSATION STARTER BANK. *"I just saw a movie that is just my kind of movie! It had exotic locations, suspense, romance and fabulous music. What's your favorite movie this year?"*

In defining a conversational style, try turning to the media for help. I liked the repartee between the husband (played by William Powell) and the wife (played by Myrna Loy) in all the classic The Thin Man movies. In each movie, Mr. and Mrs. Nick Charles solve mysteries. What I enjoy about their conversational style is their outright adoration for each other which is usually expressed in a humorous, complicated and even sarcastic verbal repartee.Their conversation style is filled with quirky, deadpan remarks and dry unconventional comments!

What's his Conversation Style?

TAKE HOME QUIZ: Rent a movie that has your favorite conversational style.Can you find a movie that is an example of the style of conversation that you want for your future husband? What style would best nurture, fortify and excite your sense of self?

The negative space in conversation is equally important to the balance.

Conversely, the person with whom you can spend time in silence is a special friend. A relationship that has traveled along the dating highway to the quiet spot, and survived, is a relationship at peace. Remember the times on a first date when there was a silence that became awkward? Think back on that embarrassing moment until someone started to speak. Usually both of you at the same time. We need someone in our lives who is graceful, grateful and comfortable with those silent times. In a good relationship, silent times are comforting and endearing, just as much as the moments filled with words.

One of my most precious memories of a date was one that I had in Mexico City. I was dating a very intelligent, witty Mexican. He was studying for his master's degree in the university and was fluent in three languages. He had the gift of creating puns and even wordplays in English. He would say silly things like, " Well, he was acting like a dog on a log." We spent one rainy evening walking along a glorious old Mexican colonial residential area. Afterwards, we ended up in a coffee shop. At first I was a little disappointed in not having a glamorous date, but I was wonderfully wrong. In the booth, as we sipped our hot chocolate for hours with the rain pouring outside, he proceeded to tell me what it felt like to be Mexican, how he viewed history from his vantage point of the lower latitude. It really stirred my soul when he talked of his pride of country and hopes for its future. The depth and new information that I gathered that night will always be with me. Of all the moments that we shared that summer, that evening of listening to his conversation was the most precious of all.

Conversation. The tuning in to another's wavelength. It can be those whispers in our ear that send an electric charge down the neck.

Whatever the context, the art of communication unravels the truth about a person.

Is he listening?

The ebb and flow of conversation includes no talk at all. Is the listening equally shared? Do you feel intimidated, bored or anxious to get a word in? Can you remember anything that was said after you have gone your separate ways? Was he listening to your words and responding in a manner that spoke to your heart? In the next encounter, did he remember anything of significance from your previous conversation?

Listening: Verb, to perceive usually by ear; hearing, attending, harking, heeding.

HEARTWORK: QUIET, PLEASE.

Step #1. Add adjectives to the list. Define your future partner's "verbal" style . Is he chatty, witty, serious?

Step #2 Define his listening style. Is he attentive, curious, deep?

Take a mental trip back and visit your best encounter with a man that involved a fascinating conversation or a simple good laugh. How did it begin? How did you feel after this event? How can you word this area of need into your want list? How was his listening style important? Include the voice, the grammar, the tone, the pitch, and the heart behind the words. How much of the conversation is given away to humor and laughter?

Think about this event and write the qualities on THE LIST.

When all is said and done, we love to come home to a good conversation about our day's events, the expectations for the future and the open ears of a good listener.

Talk is CHEAP, yet the greatest of LUXURIES!

Money matters

Speaking of money, let's explore some issues that surround the subject of money and how it relates to the search for the perfect mate. "Money" is an area that you will need to communicate about for the years to come. How important is money in the qualities of your future mate? Is it part of your absolute musts or a negotiable?

HEARTWORK: DEFINING WEALTH

Webster's Dictionary defines wealthy as: Having wealth; affluent; rich; characterized by abundance, ample; opulent.

Define how wealth plays a part in your future partnership. Add this to THE LIST.

I define wealth as: A good relationship shares similar money concerns and aspirations. For this is the place to cultivate true wealth. Each assists the other to obtain their maximum earning potential. True abundance is achieved by working together as a team to gain monetary needs. It is here that we celebrate all the things that money cannot buy: harmony, well-being, love, affection and emotional safety from the world.

Prosperity in a relationship? It is the rich soil to harvest a crop of personal creativity.

Do you realize that true prosperity means lack of money worries? As you compile THE LIST, try to consider just what are your issues and concerns about money and marriage. Do you know what you really need and how much you are willing to give?

What about you? Are you blinded by a man's wealth? Are you determined to find a man who has as much money as you do — or more? Are you placing too much emphasis on money while ignoring the rest his qualities?

✔MONEY MATTER CHECKLIST

It's been said that to know a man intimately is to read his income tax return. How open are you both to total honesty about your assets and liabilities? Consider these issues when you are ready to focus on one man. Remember, love is harder to find than prosperity.

1. **What is his general attitude about money?**
2. **Is he generous?**
3. **Is he optimistic about his monetary future?**
4. **What are his family "issues" about money?**
5. **What does he think about your spending habits?**

HEARTWORK: GET CLEAR ABOUT YOUR ATTITUDE ABOUT MONEY.

Add the information from above to THE LIST. If there are specifics that you will not tolerate, use the NO NO portion for them.

With your extensive list started, now you must be ready to enter the field to gather yet more information. GETTING OUT THERE will give you a new perspective on dating, that of enjoying it!

"Look for a sweet person. Forget rich."

Estee Lauder, Advice on Choosing a Spouse, New Yorker, 15 Sept. 1986

PART IV Go...Meeting and dating

"History may be divided into three movements: What moves rapidly, what moves slowly and what appears not to move at all."
Fernand Braudell, *New York Times*, June 76

Chapter Twelve

GETTING OUT THERE

"Don't be afraid your life will end; be afraid that it will never begin."
Grace Hansen

Now in this fourth section of the book, the focus is on meeting men. This section of the Book Entitled "GO" is dedicated to all aspects of dating. There is information on where to date, whom to date, how to enjoy dating and how to keep your heart and feelings under wraps while dating. The big secret to enjoying the dating process is keeping it short and sweet. You are not having a relationship! You are getting a quick peek at the male species. The more you date, the more information you gather about what you want in a mate. This increases your chances of finding a perfect partner.

"No one can make you feel inferior without your consent."
Eleanor Roosevelt 1884-1962

Let's break down the essentials first. You need to meet one man to find a perfect partner. The trick is that you have no idea who this will be, where you will meet him and when it will occur. So getting out there, as frequently as possible, is essential.

It would be impossible to be single without muttering at least one of these statements. Let's get these out of the way so that they do not impede your progress. Here are the myths:

Myth 1. Part A. *"There aren't any good men out there."*

Is there really a *"man shortage"*? Not really. Have you noticed how many personal ads are written by men? Many, many men put "wanting to have a meaningful relationship" as a number-one desire and the area in life that gives them the greatest sense of satisfaction. Dating services often have more men than women.

The idea that the "good ones" are taken is not true. This is one of those modern-day myths. This notion is supplemented by the jokes and comments that are out there. So don't let this untruth invade the brain and become a fact. Simply laugh and move on. One of the primary reasons to get out and mingle with the singles is simply to discover just how many nice people are out there looking too! Of course, if you never get out, there you will never know.

The world is full of good men and good women. It is packed with fun, rowdy, wild, twisted, silly, weak, strange, wonderful, interesting, caring, learned and kind men. You must weed through many to get what you want. You must converse with them to discover their hidden nature. The good guys may not be quite as visible as the egomaniacs, but they are out there!

Each day, men are becoming available through divorce, death of a spouse and changes in goals. Today could be the day that the "perfect" one for you is starting to look for his "perfect partner."

Can you be so sure that there are no great men? Have you really looked?

Myth 1 Part B. *"There aren't any good men left."*

If you believe this, then you will need to do some extra credit homework. We need to start from scratch on this myth. Think of the men you know of, who are out there looking for love. O.K., so they may not be your kind of guy, but they are out there...right? They are very wonderful, good people, aren't they? Realize they do exist and make up your mind to look for the right one for yourself. Remember...

You only need one good man, so get through the pile of rejects ASAP!

Myth No. 2 *"I don't want to meet men in bars."*

The bar excuse is so common that few dispute it. But a bar could be a wonderful private cocktail party at an exclusive resort or after a race on the water in the afternoon. One needs to find classy, quality places. The "bar" can be like an old English men's club or like an adult birthday party. Find a place that suits your personal style. What's unique about a bar is that it is where adults can go without their children, where men can go by themselves, when they have the time and it is an accepted place to meet other adults in our society. Yes, you need to be careful about which ones you frequent. But, hey, can you come up with another more universal meeting ground than that?

Bars are one of the meeting places of the twentieth century. We don't have soda fountains, ice cream socials, barn dances, cotillions or sock hops anymore. It is one place where men and women can actually concentrate on meeting each other. You are focused on checking each other out. You are away from running your errands and minding your children. You are actually dressed for the search and have allowed some time for this activity. Yes, people do meet during their aerobics classes and while buying grapefruit but this is a much more organized arena to seek out a conversation with the opposite sex. The bar scene might be a place to meet men because many, if not most, will be single. In that situation, you are dressed for the occasion so that you can let your hair down, relax and focus on this issue. It sure beats Monday night singles at the Food Mart!

Do you have any other better ideas? If you want something - are you willing to change your thinking and go through the rigors of making it happen? It's like the overweight person who complains that they want to lose weight and never lifts a finger, just a fork. Just because you frequent a watering hole does not mean that you are wicked or an alcoholic - or that he might be. Use the following story as a reference the next time you are uncomfortable about going out to a bar.

Brenda needed to get out. She was still confused about her slow, going-nowhere relationship with the heartless heart surgeon. Brenda called Trish and asked if she would help her by going out. They decided to try out a new Italian restaurant. They hung out in the bar, which had a wonderful view of the lake. They stationed themselves in the light, airy bar and proceeded to talk to just about everybody who wandered in. As quintessential summer nights go, it was one of those rare, fun, wild, silly, crazy nights. Yes, there were hangovers to nurse the next day. Brenda heard from several of the men she met that night. The following week, Trish received a call from a gentleman whom she had given her business card to. He asked her to lunch. It was the turning point of her life. This is the tale of how I met the love of my life.

Where are there the most single men, in one room, at the same time, who have their attention focused on meeting you? You will probably find that the bar scene is a very efficient use of your TIME!

Myth No.3 *"But I hate to date."*

Not to sound like your mother, but, "Eat those peas, because they are good for you! "Just because you do not like something does not make it O.K. to not do it. When I hear this excuse, it always sounds like a whiny little 12-year-old. I often feel like saying, "Oh, didn't you know you don't have to do that anymore? We have somebody to do that for you. You can just stay home and we will bring him by." Yuck!

The ideas that you have about dating are usually based on old notions and experiences and your feelings about your self at that time. I understand that you have limited time, money, energy and tolerance, but dating is the only way to start searching for your mate.

You need to search into your soul and find out why you hate to date. Often when women say that they hate to date, they also are the ones who married the first man who showed interest in them. In hindsight, is this really the best method for researching a long-term investment in anything? Even when you buy a vacuum cleaner, you look, test-drive, check out advertisements and ask for endorsements. Many women have not even gotten this far before they make a marital commitment.

DATING? Change the word to test-driving, investigating, interviewing, researching: just do it!

Myth No. 4. ***"Even if I did get out, I wouldn't know where to go."***

Let's start out right now with a homework assignment. You will need another single girlfriend to help you with this.

HEARTWORK: TEAM BRAINSTORMING WORKOUT TOPIC "WHERE ARE THEY?"

Brainstorm with a single friend. Write out every type of event, activity, gathering and social forum that might attract the guy you would like to meet. Take a quiet moment to actually visualize your kind of guy and what he would be doing in his spare time. Fill in areas for seasonal activities, spiritually replenishing areas, formal and informal sports activities, and intellectual pursuits. Try to include many activities that are free or inexpensive. Come up with at least 15 ideas. Then prioritize these. Make a pact to attend 10 of these types of events. Go together.

Make an effort to "get in the know." Start by reading papers, stopping to read those posters in windows and listening to events on the radio. Make plans. This will keep you excited about the future. I have found that the best way to ease depression is to have fun plans to be looking forward to.

You can't be depressed if you are too busy to notice!

Don't let money stop your activities! Let as many people as possible know that you are looking for meaningful activities while trying not to spend money. My uncle was an interior decorator and usually too busy with projects to attend designer showroom events and art openings, so he sent his invitations to me. I received free tickets to many sports events. If I wanted to attend something that was expensive or hard to get in, I would ask my friends with connections to the company. I would volunteer to usher or hand out food. With various girlfriends I attended well over 20 plays, concerts and events for free!

Volunteer. This is a great way to do whatever you want to do without spending money. Often it is easier to meet people when you have a function to perform. You get to meet the people behind the scenes. I have done displays for trade groups, civic functions and weddings.

Attend those extended-family events. Make an effort to attend family events. Many times I was a "date" for a friend attending an out-of-state wedding. We would make a weekend out of it, cramming as much shopping as possible in before and after the wedding.

Find time to attend different spiritual and ethnic events. Attend a christening in a different church than your own. Take part in a tea ceremony. Learn about egg dying and the Russian Orthodox Church. Spend an evening in a Buddhist temple.

Save your money for something special. When it came to a special outdoor concert, architectural tour or designer house, I would feel I could splurge. Many were for charitable causes, so the tax deductions were helpful.

Seek uplifting low-cost events. Some of the best entertainment can be found in colleges. Their art shows, plays, concerts and portfolio previews are very interesting. These are often free or offered for a nominal fee. Many churches have concerts, meditations, lectures and events on a donation basis.

Charity. What is your charity of choice? Many women have met their mates while doing a charitable act, from baby-sitting a friend's children to working in a soup kitchen. These kinds of activities can lift our soul by unburdening our intense focus on self.

Free food. Eat for free and meet others, sounds like a win-win situation! In bars and restaurants, there are happy hours to visit. There are also winery tours, cheese factories and premieres that offer food to eat and people to meet.

Brain food. Attend lectures, book signings, library talks, art films, anything that feeds your brain. What is your brain hungry to learn?

I could go on, but I think I made the point that limited thinking can really stop your progress. Everything that I did was very enriching for my soul and my mind.

Now you know why you need to get out and have ideas of where to get out. One of the reasons that we yearn for a relationship is to feel more connected to the world. Once this happens, you become renewed and more comfortable with yourself. As this confidence increases, you will reach out to people and they will reach out to you.

Take risks to gain confidence. Gain confidence and take more risks. Gain your goal by foraging through a jungle of risks.

If you do your homework and start getting out, you will be meeting men. *"DATING FINESSE,"* the next chapter, deals with the six fea
of dating and how to conquer them.

Here is My List of Activities:

- ✔ Worked as a volunteer for an international marathon race
- ✔ Attended a book signing/lecture of favorite authors
- ✔ Attended a variety of religious ceremonies
- ✔ Got free opening-day tickets for the baseball season
- ✔ Went to the car show
- ✔ Attended holiday parties given by local ad agencies
- ✔ Helped several friends move
- ✔ Attended Little League games of relatives
- ✔ Attended reunions and conferences with my parents
- ✔ Happy Hour at a bar
- ✔ Auctions
- ✔ Reunions
- ✔ Jazz concerts
- ✔ Outside concerts
- ✔ Art openings by invitations and on Gallery Thursday
- ✔ Went on a car rally
- ✔ Learned to western dance
- ✔ Went to a dude ranch
- ✔ Went hiking and frequent walks
- ✔ Picnics
- ✔ Participated in a parade and in a holiday singing contest
- ✔ Walkathons

Chapter Thirteen

DATING FINESSE

"When we do the best that we can, we never know what miracle is wrought in our life, or in the life of another."
Helen Keller, "Out of the Dark" (1913)

A funny thing happens while you are out and having fun. You start enjoying the process of meeting people. The next step is dating.

The activity of dating is essential in finding the love of your life. Your attitude can make or break this part of the process. This chapter will help you overcome your dating FEARS. There are ways to decrease the anxiety that dating can create. Your goal is to have dating finesse, which makes the process fun and worthwhile. This chapter includes some tricks and techniques that will help you gain composure. Remember - dating is the method of meeting the most men possible. Each date will get you closer to your goals of:

1. Gathering information for the LIST.
2. Gaining confidence, poise and sureness about yourself.
3. Enjoying the fun part of being single.
4. Meeting your perfect partner.

Desire + Structured Activities = Outcome.

To learn the most while enjoying the process, you must manage your fears.

FEARS ABOUT DATING

Fear #1. What if I get rejected by the person I meet?
Fear #2. What if the whole thing seems awkward?
Fear #3. What if there are strained silences during the date?
Fear #4. What if I get too nervous to enjoy the adventure of the date?
Fear #5. What if I cannot stand this person?
Fear #6. What if he is Mr. Right, but I don't recognize it?

To eliminate these fears, stop taking dating so seriously! Whi you interact, try to stand back emotionally; as this happens, "fun factor" will kick in. As you become more relaxed, you will to enjoy this time. From this more relaxed perspective, you can observe the whole scene and find enjoyment in each activity. Remember your driver's test at age 16? Did you think you would ever enjoy driving? This is true with dating: the MORE you get out and date, the easier and more fun it becomes. You must clock as many hours "behind the wheel" in the "trenches" as possible. So experience breeds confidence. Let's face these specific fears and diminish them!

Use fear to charge your motor, not flood the engine.

FEAR #1. WHAT IF I GET REJECTED BY THE PERSON I MEET?

In actuality, it should be a relief to be rejected. Why? Because it releases you to meet more and more men, which will lead you to your soul mate sooner. The idea that you are rejected has nothing to do with you. It has everything to do with him. His "issues" deal with his past, his sense of style, his sense of himself and his agenda.

How to combat REJECTION;

1. Remember that dating is a process. You are gathering information. The more information you gather, the better your "perfect" relationship will be - i.e., the more rejections, the better your future partner can be.

2. When this happens, contact somebody else who thinks you are terrific. This can be your mother or best friend. Check in with them after a rejection.

3. Try to focus on the elegance or fun of the process - i.e., point the camera lens out onto the scene and not toward your heart. Think about the beautifully decorated restaurant, the stunning sunset, the stock tips he gave you. Focus on the idea that you are out and about and not home watching TV.

4. If you really like the gentleman, feel sorry that he did not see what a wonderful person you are.

REJECTED?

Solution:**The good news about rejection: It has NOTHING to do with you not making the grade!**

Wear rejection on your sleeve like a souvenir of your valor. It indicates that you are getting closer to getting what you want!

FEAR #2. WHAT IF THE WHOLE THING SEEMS AWKWARD?

You must find ways to feel comfortable. The following pointers will elp.

1. You suggest the place to meet, one that you are familiar with. s way, you know your way around. This can be a classy bar or

fun coffee shop. Have these locations checked out and on the ready. When he calls, you can suggest the place for a date.

2. Wear clothes that feel comfortable.

3 Be organized with a notepad, business cards, perfume, change, cell phone and any other thing that makes you feel safe and collected.

4. If the drinks date goes into dinner or the coffee date goes into a walk, are you prepared for this? Do you have a coat, umbrella and so on? Is your parking meter well fed?

5. Keep the first date short. If you both like each other, get together another time.

6. Before, during or after the date, feel free to take a break and go to the rest room and give yourself a pep talk.

AWKWARD?

Solution: Be prepared to feel awkward. It's perfectly normal.

Have you ever seen an awkward Girl Scout? Be prepared.

FEAR # 3. WHAT IF THERE ARE STRAINED SILENCES DURING THE DATE?

These quiet little moments can seem deadly when you are trying to get to know someone. Yet they are bound to occur when you do not know the other person. The best way to deal with these dead spaces is to do some advance homework.

1. Always have at least five questions to ask him about himself. These can be created ahead of time by the information that you have about him. Even the smallest of clues can lead to 5 intelligent inquiries. If you know his career, find out what is of interest about it. Ask questions about his hobbies, why he lives where he does and so on. Write these down and have them on the ready if the going gets too quiet.

2. What is the latest news? Often just by scanning Time and Newsweek on your way into the restaurant, you can gain some topic starters.

3. Remember that he does not know that you are gathering information about him and men in general. Find out about HOW he thinks. Go ahead ask him about his kids, his future plans, his favorite restaurant, books, wishes, hopes and fears.

4. Ask leading questions that incorporate your passions. If you love architecture, ask him how he likes the architecture of the room. Maybe you love color and pattern, ask him how he picked his tie. If you love sports, ask him if he ever ran the St. Patrick's Day race. Get him talking about the subjects that you love.

SILENCE?

Solution: When it occurs, it has nothing to do with the

being a "failure" or not.

To eliminate silence on a date...bone up on your subject!

FEAR # 4. WHAT IF I GET TOO NERVOUS TO ENJOY THE ADVENTURE OF THE DATE?

The more you focus on this fear, the worse it will become. You may need to have a drink or go for a run before the date. You will need to find a way to unwind your mind from creating mental anxieties. Remember that he is nervous too, although you may not be able to detect it. The ideas listed below will lessen the fear and, with practice, the nervousness should diminish and the fun should kick in.

NERVOUS?

Solution: Gather techniques that work for you.

1. Being gracious and courteous is always a way to comfort any nervous soul. When you take the soothing role, the tone is set for less tension right from the beginning.

2. Allow yourself extra time. When you are meeting somebody do not be late. This means allowing extra time to get to the meeting place. If you arrive early, go the rest room, walk around the block. There is nothing worse than arriving late and frazzled because you could not find a parking spot.

3. Establish a time frame for the date. Knowing how long it will last can help alleviate nervousness.

4. Have something planned after you leave the date. Something fun! It could be a dinner with friends or some treat that you have left at home. This will give you something to look forward to.

5. Be aware of how you react under stress. Are you a hand-wringer, a finger-tapper or an interrupter? Find ways that you can prevent this, even if you have to sit on your hands or count to four before you speak. This way you won't be knocking over drinks and so forth and blurting things out. Preventing these mishaps will help you feel less nervous and more calm.

NERVOUS?

Solution: Have backup plans.

Gracious manners will always soothe the savage soul.

FEAR #5. WHAT IF I CANNOT STAND THIS PERSON?

You have met him and you cannot stand him. It doesn't matter if t is mutual or not, you need to maintain your cool and be polite. his can be a shock, and sometimes it takes time to gain your comsure. Give yourself time to settle your mind by remembering e factors.

1. You know you can endure one half hour of time with him to make sure he is not just nervous.
2. Since you do not care if you hear from him again, experiment with questions that you have not dared to ask before.
3. Hopefully, your plausible excuse is ready in hand and you do really have a nice event to go to afterwards.
4. Remember we often learn more from bad dates. Knowing what you do not want clarifies what you do want.
5. The good news is that you do not have to worry about rejection, because you can be the "rejecter" this time.

DON'T LIKE HIM?

Solution: Keep it short and sweet.

FEAR #6. WHAT IF HE IS MR. RIGHT, BUT I DON'T RECOGNIZE IT?

This is the easiest fear of all! You may not know him when you see him on this very first encounter, but by the second or third date, you will know. Do not worry, because you are getting so prepared, you won't make this mistake. The following facts will help you.

Fact One: In almost every case of couples who have found their perfect partners, they consistently made the following statements about meeting their perfect partners:

- ❑ They knew it within the first three dates.
- ❑ There was instant rapport.
- ❑ There was a consistent level of comfort with each other.

These feelings are very difficult to not notice. You will know it when you start to learn more about him and spend more time with him.

Fact Two: If he is the one for you and you do blow it on the first date, you will absolutely have more chances to meet him. Remember there are other forces at work here.

MR. RIGHT?

Solution: Experience will guide you to knowing him when you see him.

You can't blow it because you will know it.

Wardrobe!

One of the ways to gain confidence in dating is to have the right clothes. This may seem trite, but if you feel comfortable and sexy, you will have a better time. The trick is to have outfits that are comfortable and special, and that show off your body. Men like to see a woman's form. How fast can you get ready and walk out of the house feeling confident?

HEARTWORK: THREE DATING OUTFITS, LINE THEM UP AND OUT YOU GO.

Please spend some time with a friend and line up these three outfits in your closet. You may already have these clothes or need to hit the shops. They should be ready, clean and comfortable. There is nothing worse than flying home to change, only to find that that perfect outfit is at the cleaners, in the wash, or needs repair.

You may have other types of clothes for dating, but the following basic dating necessities will get you through most occasions:

1. The "Saturday morning going out for coffee" outfit. This can be used for walks, sporting events, picnics and other casual occasions.

2. The "after work for drinks" outfit. This needs to be polished, professional and yet alluring.

3. The special events ensemble: Fancy clothes for an opera, ballet, holiday party or special dinner.

When you have the right clothes, you don't have to worry about being comfortable. This will lessen the stress, and enable you to concentrate on your date. When you look great, you can focus on the process. When the stress factor drops, you will have more fun.

RULES TO LIVE BY:

Can you get ready for a date in a half hour? Many opportunities will be "spur of the moment."

A. Each outfit needs to be clean and pressed. Check the hems and seams. Don't put off doing any repair work until there isn't time.

B. Shoes. Do you have the right comfortable shoes for the outfit? If they are new, make sure that the soles have been walked on — there is nothing as embarrassing as slipping on a floor because of slippery shoes.

C. Hose. Do you have the correct nylons, unused and in the package? Do not risk using an old pair for fear of runs. That is true for footies and socks.

D. Underwear. Are you ready with the right undergarments? Do you have the strapless bra for that evening dress?

E. Purses. Do you have the right purse? Do you have all the items in the appropriate sizes to fit each occasion from an evening bag, to a belly bag to a tote?

F. Money and other stuff. Along with the right bag, you will need change for phones, cosmetics, combs, paper and pen.

G. Outerwear. Do you have the right coats and wraps for the climate? Have you tried them on with each piece to see if they hang ·ght?

Makeup. Have you had your makeup checked to see if it is up

to date and can add the maximum amount of glamour by using the minimum amount of articles?

I. Breath. Do you have a supply of breath mints for that garlic appetizer? I suggest buying a jumbo pack of the brand of your choice and planting them everywhere. There is nothing more frustrating than needing a stick of gum and having to go to a store on the way to meet somebody.

J. Your car. Is your gas tank full? You do not want to be filling the tank in your evening gown.

K. Cell phone. Is it charged and ready to go? Does it fit into your bag?

Betsy was trying things differentlyl She was dating someone who was more interested in her; he had pursued her and he had made the relationship really fun, at first. In the past, she would find a man who interested her and would try to make him notice and like her. Yet this current relationship had gone from fun to frantic. Usually, she would stick it out, hoping it would magically get better. Her usual thinking revolved around the idea that he was the only one who would ever love her. She tried to communicate about change with him but he found it impossible to find a solution. Betsy ended it. The minute she got into her house the phone rang. It was her girlfriend who wanted to go out. Betsy pulled on her great black blazer and pants and out they went. Little did she know that this night would change her life forever. She would meet the love or her life.

Add MYSTERY, DRAMA, EXCITEMENT and INTRIGUE into your life...start dating.

Next, you need to move on to ways to protect your inner self as you continue dating. Chapter Fourteen, *"KEEPING THE NUMBERS UP,"* demonstrates a sure-fire way to guarantee this.

Chapter Fourteen

KEEPING THE NUMBERS UP

"Ever tried? Ever failed? No matter. Try again. Fail better."
Samuel Beckett 1906-89

Now you are clear about WHY you need to "get out there." Next, let's formulate HOW to do this. HOW do you get to your goal in the quickest manner possible? How do you save your heart and soul from any damage? KEEPING THE NUMBERS UP is the way! This is your First Aid Kit to survive the rigors of dating. Sound too good to be true? Let's take a look at the system!

KEEPING THE NUMBERS UP means that you never look back - only forward.

The four elements of KEEPING THE NUMBERS UP are:

1. RULES OF SURVIVAL
2. MEETING AS MANY MEN AS POSSIBLE
3. BUDDY SYSTEM
4. VENTING

Think about your dating pattern. What happens to you during the dating process? What is your pattern while dating? Are you able to keep moving during this time or do you get stuck? Do you get hung up or brokenhearted and then drop out of the race to lick your wounds? Take a moment to calculate all the time you have spent recovering from the various pitfalls of dating.

Does Stacy's story sound familiar?

Stacy has been diligently dating for over a year. By attending one function each week, she has been dating a few new men per month. Her attitude about men is getting better because she now understands that there are so many great men out there. Her LIST is getting longer. It had been really fun until she met Joe.

She met him on a blind date. Stacy was amazed at how many interests they had in common. Stacy thinks that of all the men she has met, he is far and above the most wonderful. He's the first to get her blood boiling and her spirits high.

Here is the problem. *Ever since the second date, she has* *heard from Joe. Yet, when he dropped her off, he said he would call. Now it is three weeks, almost four and she is going crazy. Each time the phone rings, she hopes it is him. She even called his office to see if he was out of town, but he was still in the city. Then she called his home phone, listening to his message and hoping for a clue about him. Now she finds herself in a full-blown self-analysis marathon trying to figure out what went wrong. "What did I do wrong? Was it my hair? Was it something that I said?" and on and on. As the weeks slide by, she is getting more depressed and more desperate. If she could just talk to him to find out what went wrong, she would change whatever needs fixing.*

She feels so desperate because he is the one man that she really, really, really cared for. She thought the feeling was mutual. Now she is in a major depression and too upset, too confused and too disappointed to even get out again. It will take several months to even think about meeting another man. To add to the misery, she has called several friends to complain and now they are burned out too.

BEEP! STOP! What is wrong with this story? Everything! In fact, there are ten things wrong with this after-date behavior. Does any of the above sound familiar? Now is the time to learn the ten rules of survival from dating. Let's look back at the story to see how Stacy should have reacted after dating Joe.

RULES OF SURVIVAL

1. When a man says "I'll call you." it means only one thing: "Good night."
2. You do not call him or his machine or his office under any circumstances.
3. You do not blame yourself in any way.
4. His agenda has nothing to do with you, so do not spend a sec ond trying to figure it out.
5. You do not hear your phone. Why? Because you are not home. You are busy. You are out.
6. You feel like getting out because you have not stopped meeting men and dating. Why? Because you have not reached your goal of meeting your perfect mate.
7. The feelings must be mutual when you find the love of your life. When someone that you have dated does not call you back - you do not even stop. You move on. There is something going on in his world, not something wrong with you.
8. There is no set time when he will call back, so keep getting out there while you wait.
9. When it's right, you both know it and it is easy.

10. If you act this way, you will waste more months, years and even decades.
11. Don't burn out all your friends by calling them to complain; have a system in place.

Can you see this pattern in your life? You could be looking at a decade without reaching your goal of your perfect partner! It gets especially dangerous when you have to repair the damages that you have done to yourself by second-guessing this man's behavior. You do not have this time! Your goal is to find a man who is "perfect" for you in the least amount of time, with the most amount of knowledge.

A timesaving tip:

Spend time in a great relationship, not in second-guessing the behavior of a man you have just met.

It is time for you to administer "tough love" to yourself. This behavior of waiting around is similar to looking for a job. Do you send one resume to one company? No, you send out your resume to every company that has a job like the one you want! Often through this process you find one that is even better suited to your skills than the one you "thought" you wanted in the first place!

The closer you get to knowing what you want, the more you keep looking.

MEETING AS MANY MEN AS POSSIBLE

The process of "Keeping the Numbers Up" means that you always have several men that you are dating and several that you have met that may or may not call you back. This enables you to keep your focus on your goal, that of having fun while looking for Mr. Right. Do not focus too much on any one man. This will eliminate waiting around, while watching your self-esteem drop. It is shifting your focus away from a single person to the whole adventure of dating. So when you don't get the phone call, you are only mildly disappointed. Why? You are a little too busy to fret because you are getting ready to go out on yet another date with somebody else. So many, many fish in the sea! **Keep fishing!**

Take a numba!

While you meet other men and date many men, you are practicing the ultimate act of faith. You are expressing your knowledge that the love of your life is coming and you are willing to get out there and look. Watch out where you put the focus. If you only care about one who "seems" great but he doesn't call, you are saying that he is the only worthwhile man out there. Therefore you are doomed because he di not call. Yet, if you keep getting out there, you will save yourself t embarrassment of throwing yourself at one man. This occurs w you like a man but he doesn't seem to be quite that crazy about you. This keeps you from strange and desperate behavior to try to get feedback from him about what he feels about you. Trust me — you don't need to know! **Keep moving**!

THE BUDDY SYSTEM

Now is the time to set up the buddy system. Enlist a single friend. There is a twist, however. When you call to complain, BEWARE — you will not get any sympathy or get into a long, drawn-out analysis of the man. Surprise, surprise! You will get something like this: *"He must be blind! Well, his loss is some other man's gain. Let's get out and move on and keep the numbers up."* You will notice that there are no excuses and no digging the dirt - just a positive affirmation about how great you are. Without missing a beat, you can move on and out the door! There is no time allowed for any excuses for him or doubts about yourself and how you were perceived. Instead, you two set up a time to get out. You recover by getting out and having a good time by meeting more men. Think of the time saved by skipping the whining stage and moving on! **Stop whimpering and start simmering!**

HEARTWORK: THE BUDDY SYSTEM

Now is the time to enlist a buddy who is willing to keep you on track and get out there with you. Just like an ally who helps you keep on your diet, this friend needs to be enlisted to aid you in "Keeping the Numbers Up." Make a few phone calls and fill in the blanks below.

My Buddy is________________________________.
Phone numbers____________________________.
Time to phone_____________________________.

Here are the rules to the Buddy System.

A BUDDY stops you from any self-sabotage.
A BUDDY will not allow you to wallow in the past.
A BUDDY will initiate an action plan to a specific place or activity.
A BUDDY never gives advice. You know when they say "Let's keep the numbers up" that it is time to move forward and never look back.
A BUDDY will direct the conversation to the next outing. The time, place and clothes.

You and your BUDDY must create rules to live by. Set up guide-s for hours and frequency for going out. Talk about the times appropriate to call each other. Always establish who is driving and where to meet. Make a pact that even if you feel worn out and ugly by the established time, the show must go on. Help each other get out and not stay home with your head under the covers. Soon, when you get a call from your buddy and she says, "Hey, what are you doing Friday night? I need to get my numbers up," you'll know that you need to be a friend and get out with her.

Help each other with each other's little phobias. The "but I can't go out because I'm just too fat" kind of a stupid hang-up. Know each other's hang-up and help. My friend Molly had an absolute hang-up about her bangs. She is stunning in her fresh, natural way. She is stick-thin and tan, with white teeth — a crowd-stopper. Yet, she would fuss and fuss about her bangs. From one day to the next I never saw any difference with them, but she would stop everything and often bum herself out over the curve, length, and each little nuance of her bangs. I got into the habit of telling her, when I could see a kind a panic overcome her, that her bangs looked fine and to stop fussing. She would do the same for me. This kind of coaching is helpful during the bouts of self-loathing that accompany the kind of public viewing that goes on when you enter new terrain.

Go ahead and gripe about it, then keep moving along!

VENTING

Another keen buddy system technique is to allow time for "venting." This friendship and sanity saver is a method to help people express and release their anxiety about something in their lives. What is unique about venting is you can complain about an issue without ridicule, analysis, categorization, or input from the other party. **It basically allows to you let off steam.**

The system works like this. You set up the guidelines in advance with a friend. Things like hours that are O.K. to call. Is it O.K. to call at work, after 10 p.m. and so on? The catch is that the friend is not allowed to interrupt or edit and, most important of all, they may not give advice unless asked to by the caller. They also can never dredge up what you tell them at some later time.

HEARTWORK: VENTING PARTNERSHIP

Establish a venting partnership with a friend. This does not have to be with the same person that you have your Buddy System with. In fact, it could be a friend who has a totally different lifestyle than you do. Set up guidelines in advance.

Now, when you need to get something off your chest, you can do it simply and with the least amount of guilt. Remember tha women want to fix everything for everybody. Ironically, just a good gripe session is often the best way to deal with many issues that come our way. We often feel guilty about complaining about these issues, yet we need to validate how we feel. By venting, you keep positive energy flowing. It stops you from getting bogged down in petty issues that you really can not resolve anyway. By talking out loud, we can exorcise the negative and move on.

A typical "venting" would go something like this:

Ventor: Hi Kelly, this is Tricia.

Friend: Yeah, how is it going?

Ventor: Kelly, is this an O.K. time to do some venting?

Friend: Sure, I just put Jason to bed and I am about to load the dishwasher.

Ventor: O.K., here goes. And thanks in advance. I know that I shouldn't be going on and on about Burt. It is just that it seems so unjust that he is going to Mexico with this new girlfriend of his. I just can not get it out of my mind. I just can not believe that he ______________. O.K., I am done."

Friend: Do you want to talk about it?

Ventor: No, but thanks and goodnight.

The two techniques of the BUDDY SYSTEM and VENTING make it easy to get out and meet more men.

HEARTWORK: DOUBLE YOUR PLEASURE---MEET AS MANY MEN AS POSSIBLE!

Find one or two girlfriends who are single and want to get their numbers up. Research all the areas that are good opportunities to meet men. Look at the list and try to attend one event each week. Set up the ground rules. Make sure you have covered the basics.

Cancellation policy: Can you cancel out if you feel sick or have a date?

Time limits? No matter how the night is going - whether it is great or awful - when do you leave?

Designated driver: Who drives?

Who picks the location? Try to find as many interesting and free social events like art openings, classy bars, banquets, auctions, weddings, etc.

So get out there! Your phone can ring just as easily when you are out as when you are home!

In keeping yourself going, it is often the chin that is the most difficult to keep up!

Now you have a system to survive the meeting, dating and waiting that are integral parts of finding the love of your life. By KEEPING THE NUMBERS UP, you are guaranteed to meet your goal with the least amount of scrapes and scars. Besides, when you do meet him, you want to be in great shape, not battered mentally and emotionally.

The next chapter will enlighten you about how to protect yourself during dating. *"Millennium Dating"* deals with Dating Don'ts, when to stop dating a man and how to tell Mr. Right from Mr. Fling.

PART V.
THE FINISH LINE...Narrowing the focus

"When two people love each other; they don't look at each other; they look in the same direction."
Ginger Rogers, *I don't Want to Live Without Love*, Parade 8 Mar 87

Chapter Fifteen

MILLENNIUM DATING

"Get the advice of everybody whose advice is worth having — they are very few — and then do what you think best yourself."
Charles Stewart Parnell 1846-91

Now that you know why you must date and how to date, I assume that you are dating like mad! The following chapter is here to help you date with a new attitude. At some point, while meeting many men, you may encounter one of these situations, which I call "red flags" because they serve as a warning to you to slow down and check out the curves ahead. Dating in the new millennium requires you to be alert to the following:

✓ When dating does not become an audition, you enjoy the time.
✓ By always being truthful about yourself, you will never find yourself in a compromising position.
✓ When you like someone, you can only date him up to three times to determine if he is "the one."
✓ If you do not like him, then you need not feel guilty about not dating him again.
✓ By forcing yourself to stay in the "present" at all moments, you will not feel much pain if the relationship does not work.
✓ It is O.K. to have a romantic fling, just as long as you do not make him a candidate for the future love of your life.

By using these guidelines and not responding with the FIVE DATING points, DATING IS FUN!

The more you see - the more you know - the more you experience - the more you understand - the more you comprehend - the more you know it when you see it!

DATING DON'T #1. Don't try to force him to like you.

Dating has previously been thought of as a time to be inspected, judged and considered worthy or not. Today, that is not the case. In the past, your poor ego was exhausted from pulling out all the stops as if in an audition. In the end, the soul's true essence is what we want people to savor and discover. Yet how do we let our greatness be known? Shouldn't we work at letting our great feats and accomplishments casually slip out? No, not really.

Dating is much like being the interviewer, not the interviewee. You are the one asking the subtly probing questions, observing, sitting back and keeping the conversation going. You are directing the conversation in the direction you want it to go! You are seeking information about him. You can be in the driver's seat!

Gigi was in a funk. It had been three weeks and she had not heard from Sam. She thought that the date had gone well. She had told him about her antique car, her brother the stunt pilot, her properties all over the world, her love of race cars and car racing, her paintings that had just sold and about volunteering at the animal shelter. She knew that she really liked Sam even though she had not found out much about him. At least he knew what a great catch she was.

What is wrong with this scenario? Gigi was trying so hard to be liked that she overlooked the most important goal of her date....finding out about Sam. She never came up for air for long enough to learn about him.

Instead of trying to let the person you are dating (interviewing) know all about you, sit back and learn all about him. Watch the body language. Go ahead and read between the lines. Ask probing questions. You can be the one to decide if this person is for you. When all is said and done, you do not feel so exposed and vulnerable.

I am not advocating that you sit there and throw out question after question from a list of pre-described concerns. You need to have fun and offer some tidbits about yourself. It is just that in protecting yourself, two things happen:

A. You can sit back out of the spotlight, which helps keep you from feeling exposed.

B. You can compile a profile on the man.

When you walk away, you should be able to describe him in one sentence. "He was a kind and giving individual who has a great love of German shepherds and Western art," is one such example. When he is not Mr. Right, you will not have exposed yourself to his approval or disapproval. All you have done is had him tell you about himself and add the qualities to your list.

Learn, don't yearn.

DATING DON'T #2.

Don't present yourself as someone you are not.

We can become really miffed when we are rejected by somebody! This applies even when we don't even like that other person. So the next time, we may want to invent something about ourselves that we may feel will "improve our stock value" and up our personal ante. Do not be tempted! Never misrepresent yourself. As the future unravels, the lies will only slap you in the face! If you feel you must lie, then you need to stop dating and work more on yourself!

LIKING YOURSELF is the best defense to surviving dating!

Sassie was so excited to meet Alec. The blind date had been set up by her coworker in publishing. All the information about Alec was exciting. He was well traveled, wealthy and great-looking. Sassie was determined to make a great impression. She borrowed her brother's new Mercedes and bought a very expensive pair of shoes and matching purse. She made sure that Alec heard about her trips to Europe and even made up a story about hiring an interior designer for her condo. She wanted him to know that she was in the same league that he was in. Unfortunately, after the date was over, she never heard from him again.

What is wrong with the story? Sassie did not know that Alec was desperately seeking a woman who was not so wrapped up in the material world. He had been around so many women of that type. Besides, he felt that she was more interested in his money than in him. She seemed to want to impress him. The sad news is that Sassie was usually not focused on money, but she felt he would not like her for her non-materialistic ways. In fact, they had many interests in common. That is why his friend had set them up.

If they did go out again, Sassie would sooner or later have to reveal that she had not represented herself honestly. This would then jeopardize the relationship.

Spend time on learning about the man. Show the kind, loving, interested and nurturing adult that you are. Dating becomes an opportunity to simply "meet" another person. This will always be interesting, challenging, wonderful and even fun. When you approach the dating process from this "higher" level, most of the anxiety leaves (since it is based on worry about being judged and worry about wasting time). When you really talk to somebody, you always come away enriched. Instead of worrying about "Will he like me?," concentrat on the courage it took for this person to ask you out.

Don't seek approval, seek information!

Three strikes and he's out

DATING DON'T #3. Don't keep dating him if he is not "the one."

As you meet men, there will the ones that you know you do not wish to go out with again, the ones that you know that you really want to see again and those that you are just not sure of one way or the other. What are the rules?

It may take a few dates to really get to know a man. The first meeting is designed to be a quick "look and see." The second date and third dates are as far as you should go before you consider him to be a potential "runner-up" for the position as partner for life. Now is the time for deep thinking. This is where many women get stuck. You have somebody who likes you and you like them. Now you are enjoying the idea of a steady date. You are toying with the idea that you might bring him to an office function next week and then there are those tickets to the opera next month. STOP!

After the third date, ask yourself, *"Is this the perfect mate for me?" It is a big mistake to dive into any relationship that does not have the potential for being "the perfect one." How do you know? By reviewing THE LIST.*

Cyndy was amazed and horrified. For the last decade, she had developed a dating and relationship pattern. She would meet a man and by the time they had dated only four times, they were an item. She never dated several men at once, or one for a short term. She never had a chance to narrow the choices and decide on one. Instead she would work and work at making this relationship work. Usually they would stay together for about two years and then the breakup would occur. She would be devastated because she had worked so hard at the relationship. Sadly, it would often take her up to a year to recover. Then she would go out and meet another man and this pattern would start over again.

What is Cyndy doing wrong? She is not checking out what is out there. She is not clearly defining what she wants. She is not respecting herself enough to know that a great one will come after she becomes clear about what she wants. When it is right, she will not have to work so hard. She is wasting years in dating the wrong men and years in recovery time.

Remember that the first date/meeting is a tension-filled situation for both parties. Often the next date is actually fun because the stress is lessened. Yet if you are sure he's not the "one," then do not go out with him again. If you are not sure, give it one or two more tries.

DATING DON'T #4. Don't "future jump."

When you "future jump," you mentally move into the future with little regard to the present. This means that you have not gathered enough evidence, yet you are acting as if certain things have already been said or done. An example might be:

You are on a date with a man who has a fun new sports utility vehicle. This is the second date and it is in the Spring. You are thinking that it would really be fun to go skiing with him in the Winter. Your mind shows you images of him helping you put your ski boots on and the two of your sipping cocoa in the ski lodge. Stop! This is not good. It is a bad idea for many reasons. Here are a few:

1. Stay focused on the present. You are still observing on this second date.

2. You are creating a mental image of this man based on imaginary images.

3. If this relationship is not the one, then you will not only mourn its demise but also that of the future that you have projected. You cannot afford to waste the time and emotions on things that never were.

Many sad moments occur when you mourn the loss of a relationship. Yet we often have added extra sorrow because of the loss of all of these illusions as well. You must stay in the "now" all the time. This will keep you from dating somebody because of his "potential." It will keep you from dating over the three-date limit. It will keep you focused on what you really want in a long-term relationship. Today's reality is all that counts.

If you spend your time thinking about the future with this man, then the present must not be very engaging.

Why isn't Mr. Fling really Mr. Potential?

DATING DON'T #5. Don't confuse Mr. Fling with Mr. Potential.

There will come a time when you meet the most sexy, good-looking, engaging, fun gentleman. You are crazy for him! You two hit it off and it is paradise. You don't care about the dating etiquette, the third date or whatever. You dive in and have a fling! It is too grand! You want this wonderfulness to last forever. You want this man to be Mr. Potential. Only he is unavailable. He is not interested in a long-term relationship. He wants to keep things light. Ouch! You have just met Mr. Fling!

Who is Mister Fling? He is the flirt who has a master's degree in being a sexy guy. Yes, he is good in all the wonderful romantic gestures. Yes, he really seems to focus on you and yes, he is so darn good-looking. Even though you think that you are the only woman who has discovered this about him - you are wrong. He is a professional schmoozer.

Guess what, I think he IS just the ticket for a fun time! Go for it. Just do not get all focused on turning him into your long-term partner. He is not available. Chances are, he has already told you this in so many subtle ways. It is just that you were so bowled over in the romantic flow that you didn't quite hear the "I don't want to settle down" comments he was whispering in your ear.

Patsy met Jason at an out-of-town wedding. When Jason asked her to dance, she was dazed by his Cary Grant demeanor and smile. They danced and talked and danced and walked. She felt as if she were in a movie. Their conversation seemed to zing back and forth in a witty repartee. Soon, they found themselves kissing and laughing. The night was truly touched with magic. She met him the next night and after a romantic dinner, the fireworks began again. It was a night that Patsy will never forget. The next day, Patsy flew back home with stars in her eyes and a very broad smile. Jason had been very specific — he loved her company but he did not want a long-term relationship or a long-distance relationship. Patsy could not get him off her mind. Didn't he realize that it had been years since she had connected so well with a man — if ever? Didn't he realize that they had a very special relationship? Yet when she called him, he seemed remote. She hung up and realized that he had meant what he said. She needed to move on. She felt depressed, then she became joyful. If there was one man who dazzled her so much, then there had to be another who realized just how special she was! It was time to meet as many men as possible and find him!

What is the message? Patsy started to understand the difference between a fling and a long-term partnership. She never got the two mixed up again. The fling is for romantic fun only, not the beginning of a long-term relationship. It is O.K. to have an occasional fling — just don't confuse him with your long-term committed partner candidates.

By keeping these No-No's in mind, you can move rapidly to your destination. As you reach your goal, are there still some illusions to be cautious of? Can you really trust yourself when you do meet the love of your life? What are the rules of romance? In the final part of the book, THE FINISH LINE, you will become acquainted with the answers to these questions.

A GOOD READ!

Read about Mr. Fling in Elinor Lipman's book entitled *"The Ladies Man."*

Chapter Sixteen

ILLUSIONS

"Wisdom is knowing when you can't be wise."
Paul Engle, Poems In Praise (1959)

It is just a matter of time before the love of your life appears. Are you fully prepared for this event? After spending so much time getting "out there," can you steer clear all the way to the finish? Let's review the "pitfalls" to the final stages of finding the love of your life. Let's call this a REALITY CHECK.

Fantasy vs. reality

This chapter takes a look at myths about love, marriage and life when Mr. Right appears. Do you have mixed messages from childhood and the media? Could any of these block the path to a productive and enriching relationship?

The trouble with fantasy is that it is not reality. The trouble with reality is that it isn't fantasy.

According to Webster's New Collegiate Dictionary: *An ILLUSION is an unreal or misleading image, a deceptive appearance, a misconception that fails to give the true character of the object perceived.*

In our culture, we are constantly given illusions involving love, marriage and beauty. The media with its musical lyrics, movies and television send us one consistent message. Its essence is that love creates a great marriage and life is perfect from then on. Furthermore, this happiness will last forever without any maintenance. Yikes!

Let us explore some of the myths that may cause you grief when you meet the love of your life.

THE SIX ILLUSIONS ABOUT YOU AND THE LOVE OF YOUR LIFE:

ILLUSION #1 YOU WILL RECOGNIZE HIM INSTANTLY WHEN YOU SEE HIM.

In compiling this book, I interviewed hundreds of committed couples. In almost every case, in the beginning of the relationship, they emphasized the ease of the connection. Over and over, they claimed that from the beginning:

1. It was easy and comfortable when they were together.

2. It was as if they had known each other all of their lives. Yet there was so much more they wanted to know about the other person. They had a keen interest in hearing all about the other's life.

3. It was very obvious to both parties that this was "the relationship."

Yes, you will know that this is your perfect mate quite quickly, when you have done your homework! The illusion lies in the idea that he is discernible from a great distance and by sight alone. In other words, "love at first sight." In reality, the happy couples spent time talking and being together, before this idea flashed across their collective brains. In a few cases, the two were not even especially taken with each other at the very first sighting, but after spending time together, the magic began. It takes TIME to allow this person into your space and TIME to listen and converse. The recognition comes from the gut, not solely from the eyes!

Maybe it's because I fell in love with the back of my first husband at the bank, but this "love at first sight" is a little scary. It must have been a past-life recognition with Karma to pay, because the devastation of the divorce lasted much longer than the courtship and marriage.

Yet the opposite can occur.

The time was the '60s and a shy young man watches a group of laughing college girls at a dance. He waits several dances until he asks her to dance. When they get to the dance floor, it is quite obvious that she is not just tall, but a good foot taller than he is. He is swept up with her bubbly personality. She is open to anything and decides to check this short guy out. They go on several dates and he adores everything about her. She's gregarious, he's soft-spoken. She is from a large family, he is an only child. She is from the city and he grew up in the country. Yet they have everything in common about what they want in the future. They marry, have five boys, they both become doctors. Their life combines a city/country life full of noise, laughter and fun.

Another mistake is falling in love first and then deciding how compatible you are. It should be the other way around. You must "feel" the compatibility and then the love will follow.

TRUTH: If I am going to be with him all the rest of my life, there is absolutely no rush.

Impulse buying is fine for the bargain of the week, but for a marriage, you need to slow down and investigate.

ILLUSION #2. LOVE CONQUERS ALL.

As an adult woman, you know all about love. You know what it can do and what it can not do. The illusion is that when you are in love, things go along so peacefully. The shock is when "real life" rears its ugly head. Way deep inside you may feel that "Now that somebody loves me, life will be perfect!" Or "Maybe some of this rotten stuff will not happen now that I have found this great partnership." Even as adults, we can get swept up in the euphoria of being in love.

My parents traveled to New York City on their honeymoon. They splurged on a nice hotel. They grabbed their carry-on bags and headed for the room. They parked the car in the hotel garage. When my father went down to get the rest of their things, he found the trunk empty. All of their clothes, wedding gifts and my father's naval uniforms were gone

Love is great, but reality is always happening. It is important to not sabotage these great times, yet one needs to realize that the world still moves on. It can be a real shock to have some problem arise and realize that love will not take care of the pain and discomfort caused by this event. You still have to get out into the world and deal with other people, places and things. Yes, it is easier with a loved one by your side, but the house still needs painting and your boss is still a nut case.

TRUTH: Life happens to us while love surrounds us.

ILLUSION #3. BAGGAGE CHECK. FIND A MAN WITHOUT ANY BAGGAGE.

When dreaming of the perfect mate, we tend to dream of this wonderful human being who will be everything to you. If you have a vivid imagination, you may picture him looking like the actor of the week, with a heart of gold and stars in his eyes only for you. He has no issues, problems or a past. Reality will quickly clear up the fog. Change your picture to a handsome man who is dragging his suitcase behind him. It might be a small black bag on wheels or a heavy bulky dark green trunk. This metaphorical vision relates to what EMOTIONAL, ECONOMICAL and PHYSICAL issues he has. What is he dealing with now? What is he recovering from in the past? What will he always be dealing with?

What you may consider to be "heavy baggage," others will label "just life." Are you prepared to deal with his ex-wife, stepchildren, debts, college tuition, health issues, personality flaws, hobbies, habits, attitude towards money and other issues? Are any of these included in THE LIST as your No-No's?

You may have to put up with a jealous stepchild. I have a friend who found every article of clothing in her closet cut with scissors from a spiteful stepdaughter.

The question is, What kind of dirty laundry are you willing to sort through? There is not a soul around who doesn't have issues and all the wonderful dynamics that go along with them. We are learning and growing throughout this lifetime. No one goes through it unscathed.

Your duty to yourself is to be firm about what you will tolerate and what is inexcusable. So before you jump, be clear on what could be called your bag of issues. How much should be disclosed? One learns through taking time to get to know someone; that way, very few things are taken for granted.

TRUTH: **We all have baggage the day we leave home for adulthood. It is our declaration of independence.**

The issue of the frog turning into the prince or the prince turning into the frog will always be there to haunt us during our dating days.

ILLUSION #4. MARRIAGE IS GOING TO BE BETTER THAN BEING SINGLE.

Embrace SINGLEHOOD! It won't last forever. Believe it or not, you just might miss parts of it when it is over. The days of being single are equally the precious times too! Amazingly, the times of suspense and fun are the makings of wonderful memories. When you look back at your life, these may be the good old days.

This dating process offers us a full range of activities that we may not experience later. In the end, we find that we actually enjoyed the tension, stress, letdowns, and excitement of the dating adventure.

Looking back, one is able to see what a fun and endearing time this was. The time with your girlfriends is something that may never come again. The dating scene is filled with fun, laughter and special memories. Although, during the actual events, we often are too focused on finding "him" to really embrace the fun.

I now look back at my decade of being single with nostalgia. From this perspective, there seems to be an ebb and flow to all the activities and the variety of friends I spent time with. We had so many fun lunches, walks and talks. At that time, there seemed to be "too much" time to read, work on the garden, shop and wander. These are luxuries now.

Some people realize that the thrill of the hunt is just what they want. At the end of the safari, they should go ahead and sign up for the next trip. The daily routine of marriage includes compromise, communication, boredom and even lackluster moments of silence. To some, this can seem overwhelming and just plain spooky. These women thrive on the thrill, not the routine. Others may see the invasion of another person into their private world as an insurmountable threat. The lucky ones know this about themselves and live their lives with this honest notion about their need for privacy. If you are a passion-seeker and an addict to romance - you need to consider the road of many short-term relationships. The long hard road of one long-term partner will only strike terror in your heart.

This is why you need to fully embrace the full spectrum of dating, so that you will not be tempted to yearn for it. It is better to have experienced it so fully that you do not want to go there again.

TRUTH: You may be living the "good old days" now. There is a sweetness and simplicity and joy in being single. When you are married and viewing your singlehood from another vantage point, you may be surprised at what a wonderful time it was.

The old meets the new

ILLUSION #5. EVERYONE WILL BE SO HAPPY FOR ME NOW THAT I HAVE FOUND MY PERFECT MATE.

You've found each other and life seems so sweet. Oh, but wait! There are those who are not happy about this! Be prepared for a few surprises — some will view your gain as their loss. This can be a friend, relative or your child. All feel slighted because they know that their time with you will be limited as the new partner arrives.

An example could be if you have been divorced, others may be apprehensive of this new man, because they want to protect you from another trauma. If you are true to THE LIST, this confirms your connection to him. This will help you defend why this relationship is good for you and therefore good for all concerned. Be prepared to defend yourself and the love of your life.

In Patti's case, her "friend" Janice of ten years started to act strangely. When Patti called her about the engagement, Janice sabotaged her glee by coming up with strange comments about how he proposed and what exactly he said. The day of Patti's engagement party, Janice created a big fight which left her sickened. It was at this point, while driving out the celebration, that her fiancé mentioned that Janice had phoned him to warm him about why she felt Patti's first marriage had not worked out. He was strong and had known in advance that Janice would be jealous and would probably act out from losing one of her main friends. Patti was devastated because of the breach of confidence, for planting the seed of doubt in her fiancé's mind and for such negativity on one of her most happy day

Patti should have been more prepared for this type of behavior. S was so wrapped up in her own personal glee. By realizing that oth are affected by this change, she could have avoided much sorrow.

Everyone in your life is affected by the changes of your life. While you have never been happier, others may feel slighted, used, sad, even jealous. The trick is that they will not come out and say what is bothering them. Change affects everybody differently. Marriage is a big change. So be ready for attitudes that you were not prepared for.

TRUTH: Some people in your life will feel threatened and angry as you change your life for the relationship.

ILLUSION #6. LIFE WILL BE SO EASY NOW THAT I HAVE FOUND MY PERFECT MATE.

If anything, life gets much more complex. Now you have your life to mesh with a whole other life. That's complicated! Right after I got married, I moved with my husband to another state. It might as well have been another planet because the climate was so different. Once encamped, I received a terrible shock! My life was still complicated and I still had so many issues. I was still concerned about my career, money, energy and health. It was just that now I was driving around in 114-degree weather instead of rain!

So the reality is...Life still happens! Now you have another full-time concern...the health and happiness of another person. Marriage brings change, and stress is there to meet you. Yes, it is so much easier to have a friend encamped in your home, and yes, you can even delegate some matters his way, but issues will come. The biggest depression may come once all the wonderfulness of dating, romance, engagement, marriage and the honeymoon are over. Be ready for the Three C's: COMPROMISE, CRAMPED QUARTERS AND CLUTTER.

After being single and having things pretty much as you like them, you may be in for shock. Having a new person around may be wonderful yet disruptive. Any type of change is stressing - whether its source is positive or negative. The time needed to maintain the relationship is another factor. Now you rush to the grocery store after work to make a nice dinner each night instead of eating Lean Cuisine over the sink.

TRUTH: Relationships take time and energy.

Sooner or later REALITY rears its ugly head!

Now you are becoming clear about any illusions around marriage and the perfect mate. It is imperative to find out what other illusions you may have. Why? Because these illusions can sabotage your new relationship.

HEARTWORK: REALITY AND FANTASY

There is reality and there is fantasy. What issue are you holding close to your heart that may be a challenge to the reality of life with a new partner? If you can not think of one, ask a married friend what she/he overlooked and was surprised about once the marriage began. Take out a pen and write it out. List three ways to not become entangled with this untruth.

An example might be; *"I thought my house would stay clean and neat and he would clean up after himself. The house is full of magazines and newspapers."* Truth: Life does get complicated, messy and noisy when there is a male living in it full-time. What to do? Embrace the mess. Life is complex when you are in a relationship. I'd rather have noise and mess and a partner, than quiet and neat and be alone.

____

____

____

Each life presents its own perplexities. Where do we go for help to these deeply emotional questions? How do we trust our own judgment? How do we stop relying on others and just "know"? Let's move ahead to Chapter Seventeen on *"Gut Level Information."*

Chapter Seventeen

GUT LEVEL INFORMATION

"Nothing we use or hear or touch can be expressed in words that equal what is given by the senses."
Hannah Arendt, New Yorker, 12 Sept 1970

When you meet your perfect mate, you will know it! Deep down inside and all the way through your body, you will know that he is the one. The feeling of "rightness" combined with all the hard facts collected from actual experience will be your tandem guides to the truth. By combining the formidable truth with your internal compass, you can not lose.

Be your own detective who solves that great mystery — finding the love of your life.

All the great detectives know how this works. First, one gathers the evidence. All the senses are employed to dig out the facts. Nothing stands in the way of searching out every little detail. As each small clue is meticulously sought out, one never jumps to a hypothesis. A composite grows as clues begin to reveal the true story. Often, even after a verdict has been presented, the detective has an "uneasy" feeling. Something is not right. This "unquiet" leads to deeper digging for more information. Then a new direction is taken. Frequently, the detective does not like where he is going. Yet, the TRUTH is all that matters. Finally, when all is revealed and it feels right, justice is served.

Facts + Gut Information = TRUTH with a sense of calm.

Your gut kicks in, when logic and intellect are on overload. You must stay unbiased until every detail is confirmed by your inner knowing, no matter how much you want it! You can not risk jumping to a conclusion before all the evidence is in. Below is a story of a woman who used her intuition and, with determination and persistence, found the truth.

When I asked Sam how she met her husband, she replie[d] "Well, you might say that I picked him up in a bar!" Sam is of those amazing women. She is a leader in the field of motivation. She is in demand for her effortless, fun style. She had been engaged and right as the wedding plans were getting formulated, her gut said that this was not the right man for her. She broke the engagement. One night a friend asked her out for a drink. While at the bar, she spun around on her stool and there over by a jukebox in a bright yellow light was the image of an old flame named Wes. When she went over to say hello, he was not there. The next morning, she started to call around town and could not find him. She could not stop trying to understand why this "vision" had appeared. She could not let it rest. She decided to contact his family. This was difficult, as he was from England. Yet, she managed to track down his sister in Scotland and then his mother in Holland. Finally, she reached his grandfather in London. Wes was there and the first words out of his mouth were, "You will not believe this, but I was just thinking about you. In fact, I am holding a photo of you in my hand right now." Instantly, Sam knew that her gut had led her in the right direction.

In interviewing couples in great relationships, one fact is consistent. Both parties knew that this was "it" very early on. They listened to their intuition which, when combined with their past experience, "told" them internally that this was the right relationship for them.

There is such a big difference between wanting a relationship to work and knowing that this is the one.

The truth resonates from deep inside. Rarely do those in great relationships suffer from restless nights or second-guessing. Instead, there is a sense of calm. So the intellectual mind is stopped in its tracks and there is peace instead. It is as if your whole being and the whole universe are smiling with their approval. What remains is a sense of "no rush." This combines with inner knowing that "this is the one."

One reaches a calm state when one overrides the information of the brain by fielding information from the gut. Our brain is overloaded with information gathered from our past. We must lean on an internal tracking device that is driven by ageless wisdom of a more spiritual foundation. This chapter is designed for you to test-drive your inner knowing device. I call this simply "the gut."

Don't travel in this terrain without your internal compass.

We are on a journey of the soul. This soul of ours has been around the world in many more than 90 lifetimes. This inner guide knows what we need to accomplish in this lifetime and who will help us accomplish this. It is able to recognize other souls that we have been in contact with from the past. The soul is there to aid in your search for the perfect partner.

Do I think we should only look for our soul mate? Yes and no. I believe there are many partners available for us. To say that the only enriching relationship is with a certain soul mate is too limiting. There are many men who would fit the perfect partner profile. Should we seek those men with whom we have Karma? Yes and no. Karma deals with debts that one owes, good and bad from this lifetime and past lives. We need to concentrate on attracting relationships that will only bring harmony, peace and prosperity.

The better definition for "soul mate" is someone that your gut (voice of the soul) has connected with in a positive way to create a match made in heaven.

How to know "it."

You are the only one who can clearly know the truth. There is such a big difference between wanting a relationship to work and knowing that it is the one.

When it truly is "the one":

A. You experience a sense of peace.

When the man you meet is truly the love of your life, one rarely suffers from restless nights or second-guessing. Instead, there is a sense of calm. There is certainty, no second-guessing or confusion. Your whole being will know this is right, CREATING a sense of peace.

B. You are not making it work.

We often get confused when we want a relationship to work out. We force our brain to justify this need. Yet, deep inside, there is information to the contrary. The brain overrides any red flags by frantically going about "making" this thing work. This chaotic activity can make us feel as if we are actively engaged in the process. Yet all along, we are forcing the situation. It takes experience to differentiate between rationalization and the knowledge that this is right.

C. You do not feel frantic.

It is as if your whole being and the whole universe are smiling with their approval. Yet, an atmosphere of "no rush "should prevail. When it is not right, it takes energy to push and work to make it right. All this urgent activity keeps you so busy that you overrid what the inner voice is telling you. There is a big difference between rushing to make it right and a rush from being right. You do not feel urgent when it is right, and this gives you a chance to hear what your gut is telling you.

Where do you feel what you are feeling about what you are experiencing?

You need to get in touch with your gut. Much can be gained by tuning in to our internal information sensor. How many times have you said, "Oh I wish I had listened to my gut" or "I am so glad because I had this hunch"? When seeking a mate for life, you will need to rely on this. Take this time to evaluate your past experiences with this inner knowing.

The idea of ESP is similar — the more you acknowledge its presence, the more you will have it available. How many times in your life did you listen to your brain instead of your gut and wished you hadn't? This seems especially true in love. When the brain decides it "loves" another, trouble can occur. We rush ahead and try to justify this information rather than letting the situation take its course. We have all experienced those times when we "thought" we fell in love and wound up with miserable results. It's time to have an inner knowing about the love of our life.

You just know, you know!

HEARTWORK: IDENTIFYING YOUR INTERNAL COMPASS

Describe a time in your life when you bypassed the information from your brain and listened to the voice within and, in doing so, good things happened.

An example might be:

____

____

____

There was a time in my life when I was trying out all sorts of jobs in hopes of finding a new career path. At one point I was offered a job, yet I thought I should not take it. The job was such a departure from my past experience that my brain said I would fail. So I declined the offer. As I drove home, my inner voice kept telling me to take the position. All night my gut said "Take the job!" while my brain said "This is crazy!" The next morning, I called the company back and said that I had changed my mind . Thank goodness, the job was still available to me. That phone call changed my life. This was an excellent new career path.

Now that you have completed the homework, try to locate your "gut" level area. Rethink this event that you wrote about. What did it feel like to use this navigational tool? Can you find an area in your life right now where your gut might hold the answer?

Free falling is listening to your inner voice and quietly following its advice.

Try to use your gut a little every day. The more you use it, the clearer it will become. Think about your first impression with various people. What did you "think" about someone at first? What was your "gut" feeling at first and how did this person "live up" to your inner reaction to them?

The gut is the voice of ancient wisdom from your soul.

It is essential to test your gut in matters about people. We can override the truth by what we see or what we want. We can get into trouble when we add and delete information because our brain wishes to have a particular outcome. Use your gut to find out what is really going on.

I believe that the voice of our soul is our gut. It is guiding us toward all matters that are healthy for the development of our mission during this lifetime. When we allow the "voice" to speak, we are guided to great adventures and awareness that are directions for the advancement of our soul. When seeking the love of a lifetime, our gut information draws from ancient wisdom.

Practice accessing your gut level. Use the following exercise to learn to "read" your gut.

A. Think about an issue in your life that is disturbing.
B. Sit quietly and ask your gut, "Why is this occurring in my life right now?"
C. Ignore the quick answers coming from your brain.
D. Did you get an answer or a feeling?
E. Where on your body did you feel this information coming from?
F. Practice every day for several weeks.
G. Write down the information that you have received from your gut and compare how different it is from what your brain tells you.

Often we receive a simple word. Go to the dictionary and lo

up this word. Don't judge this information. Accept it and know that the nature of this information will be revealed. You may receive an image. Break this down into analytical parts. You may see yourself walking over a bridge. Could this mean you are making a transition from something old to a new place?

Do not consult others. Soon it will be revealed to you if the gut information shed light on the truth. Pay close attention to where on your body the information came from. Are you able to identity this information as different from the answers collected from your brain? Soon, if you are not already relying on your gut for answers, you will have a new tool for instant information.

Trust your heart, then your head, and then double-check it with your gut!

Nancy visited a counselor when her 30-year marriage came to an end. She learned about meditation and inner listening to use for guidance. She started to rely on her inner listening in many small ways. One day her son-in-law asked if she would like to meet his mentor from work. This man was a widower and her son-in-law could not say enough great things about him. Her first instinct was to say "no." Her brain quickly listed why this would not work. It was too complicated and, when it did not work, this would make it uncomfortable for her daughter and son-in-law. She was still recovering from her long and miserable marriage and was resisting dealing with the issue of dating. Yet she took some time to inner listen and she received the words "comforting and comical." She decided to go for it. On first meeting him, they hit it off. She could really be herself and her shell started to lift. She hadn't laughed this hard in years. This man treated her with such respect, while her first husband had acted like she was hired help. Things only got better, as he had loads of money and wanted her to really enjoy things she had not had before. They were married 5 months later.

I use my inner voice on many issues. The information comes in around my stomach region and the tightening nerves are indicators of something to pay attention to. I can meditate on the issue and hear words and answers to my questions. I know the responses that I receive are from another part of my anatomy than my brain. Often the vocabulary and the level of information is not of my usual repertoire. There may be words and phrases that I have not uttered before. This technique is called inner listening. Keep listening to the vocabulary and sentence structure. Are they part of your usual way of speaking?

Often it's better to do something that just feels right than ask permission from others.

Practicing inner listening to your gut

It is up to you to find the best way access your inner voice. Excellent results come from being in nature. When you are in nature, take time out to stop and be still — surprising images and input can be discovered. It helps to be in a relaxed state. Ask for guidance and help.

The more you practice inner listening, the more readily the information is available to you.

You need to trust this source of information. The more you use this, the greater the insights. Ultimately you will be using your brain, intuition and gut to judge situations that arise while dating. Accept nothing that does not feel right.

Your heart has a say in the matter.

If you need answers to your emotional questions, remember that this is food for your soul. The heart can help with issues of dedication, inspiration, hope, trust and what is best for us. The heart taps into the soul and resonates with the "truth." Are you getting goosebumps? Are you feeling something in your heart? These are the indicators of truth.

Perhaps you need to "change your mind" because something is gnawing at you. Allow yourself time to make a decision. When you have found the love of your life, can you say, "I know in my heart of hearts that he is the one for me"? This along with telling others exactly why he is good for you will reassure those around you.

I had to do this with several friends and relatives when I met my future husband. They knew he had few material possessions, yet I knew that he had possessed houses and cars. He had suffered losses that would make most people never want to try again. They did not know that he had declared his love to me and how it had motivated him to go for his dreams.

Therefore it was my job to apprise them of his merits. I felt so confident, and every time I would start getting worried from what my brain was saying, I would stop and listen to my gut. Each time, I got an unstoppable flag of approval. I was reminded that he is the most kind, loving, intelligent and worthwhile person of impec[illegible] cable values that I had ever met. They pointed out his consist[illegible] love for me which was so easy and powerful. Today he is ach[illegible] ing all of his material goals that he set out to do. My inner [illegible] ance reminded me that material wealth was available at an[illegible] but loving companionship was priceless and more valuable than anything that money could buy.

You have a valuable tool to use in your search for your perfect mate. Please read Chapter 18 and make sure that you're still on track in the romance department. This next chapter allows you to explore the five rules of romance and test-drive your readiness for commitment.

Chapter Eighteen

ROMANCE

"Love is or it ain't. Thin love ain't love at all."
Toni Morrison

After all your hard work, romance has finally appeared. This is a wonderful reward for time spent gathering information during the dating process. You never stopped until you felt that you had encountered Mr. Right. Should you still be cautious? Yes!

What are the five rules of romance?

Now is the time to have fun...right? Right! But with a few little rules to live by. Well, actually, five little rules to tuck into your belt as you get out there and have a ball. They are full of suggestions to move into a committed relationship with the least amount of trauma.

RULE #1. GO SLOW!

1. **What's the rush?** We rush from one goal to the next. How much of the journey have you slowed down enough to enjoy? We rush from the engagement to the wedding to the honeymoon, and barely have time to stop and simply enjoy. ***Participate in the moments.***

2. **Pacing**. Keep your eyes focused just to the next episode. Do not skip ahead to the next chapter. Saturate all of your senses in each activity. Remember to take a mental Polaroid of these moments. Remember how you felt as a child on your birthday? All those presents to open, yet once they were opened, the thrill sort of slipped. ***Today holds all the information that you need.***

3. **Don't get ahead of yourself.** Take the time to check in with yourself. When you get home after spending time with him, do you feel content, anxious or relieved? ***Check in with yourself.***

4. **Don't rush to the altar.** Peer pressure can make us embrace someone who may not be the perfect mate. The stress of your friends getting engaged, getting married and having babies can add fuel to your search. It can make you rush into the wrong relationship. It is essential that you know that everyone has their ow timing in life. There isn't a universal time for every event to happ

to everyone at the same time. ***Embrace your own timing!***

RULE #2. ENJOY THIS TIME.

1. **Stop worrying about WHERE it's going and focus on HOW it's going.** If you feel that you need to rush to catch up, please assess your motives. One way to tell is if you are too anxious to focus on the present moment. Are you always feeling the need to push this relationship faster and farther? Don't sabotage what is wonderful today by discounting it. Keep checking how you are feeling. This is the fun part NOW!
2. **Dive in!** If ever there was a time to indulge in your romantic dreams and wishes, this is the time. Take out that purple silk robe and enjoy it because now is the time.
3. **Remove yourself from reality.** This is your time to bond. Find a place to go that is away from children, work and responsibilities. This bonding is essential in forming a strong foundation for the future. Once your lives take off, this quality time may not be accessible.
4. **Create unforgettable memories.** One can often live on great memories. Especially when you are savoring them at the time. Be romantic, dramatic and sentimental now. These are the memories that you will look back on as the decades race by.

RULE #3. STAY LEVEL-HEADED.

1. **Keep probing.** Do not forget that you are still gathering information.
2. **Hear any "little voices" in your head?** Keep track of the little red flags that flash in front of your face. Now is not the time to panic, but take note and deal with them later. Bring them up when the romance is settling down and there is time to really get clarification on it.
3. **Pull out the list.** Remember you are still in the process of discovery. Is this man going to go from boyfriend to future husband?

HEARTWORK: PULL OUT THE LIST.

Take out your list and spend some time putting a number by each characteristic. This number can have a grade of 1 to 5 in accordance with the degree of importance. For example, if you had written down that he should be a professional, and he turns out to be an accountant, then add 5 by this characteristic. Add these points up. This will give him a "grade." Is his score around 80%? What areas are still uncharted terrain? Find out what his response is to characteristics that you have little or no information on. Remember, without exception, he must match your "one-word description" and must not have any of your three "No-No" qualities.

RULE #4. KEEP PLAYING EVEN IF IT COOLS DOWN.

1. When your knees stop a-knockin', your heart should still be poundin'. As the intoxicating, passionate thrilling aspects start

to fade out, you should still feel excited and in love with this man.

2. Understand the process. This romantic time has been there for many reasons. When you are seeking your life mate, the material that is unraveled in this segment allows to you experience the sensual, sexual and passionate nature of him. This can be a revealing time for you to learn more about him and to better understand yourself.

3. Can you trade in the razzmatazz for the humdrum? Sooner or later you both will need to get back to the everyday. How are you two as a team?

Or are you a romance junkie?

RULE #5. CHECK TO SEE IF YOU ARE A ROMANCE JUNKIE.

1. Are you constantly craving the suspense and drama of dating? If you desire the heart-shaped Valentine to arrive more than once per year, then the monogamous relationship simply will not do. A long-term relationship can be romantic, but it does not thrive on just romance. It deals with the everyday living issues. If you need romance each day, then marriage will not fill the bill for you.

2. Do you feel that this romantic stage should last forever? Most people have a romantic courtship and then settle in to a simpler, more sustaining relationship. This then allows the individuals to "get on with it."

3. Does the prospect of working at romance seem depressing? Yes, you both can have romantic moments, and make efforts to enliven your relationship with romantic gestures of gifts both verbal and physical. The truth is that the dazzling, heart-piercing, brain-numbing, passionate, embracing, thrill-seeking route can not be driven down daily. Both parties need to work at romance in everyday relationships.

Romance is the flint to ignite the possibility of a long-burning flame.

One would probably die early of exhaustion and emotional confusion if this form of "romance" could be sustained for a long period of time. Romance is nature's way of enticing the sexes to get up close and personal. It is the icing on the cake of courtship. Long sustained relationships are a tribute to common goals, clear communication, self-sacrifice, humor, love, companionship, energy, giving and lots more. This stuff of life is the nutritional fodder of sustaining a relationship. Then the couple has the opportunity for creating a stable environment where children can be added and work can be pursued. The day-to-day great relationship is filled with the simple pleasures of happiness, caring, peace, safety, endearments, sex and contentment.

When writing THE LIST, think about how it will feel without

the romantic fuss and, in its place, calm security. True love is an alliance between two people to create an environment of endurance based on mutual respect, advocacy and deep caring with romance as one of the many ingredients.

When entering a long-term relationship, don your comfortable work clothes and leave the party outfits in the closet.

Are you ready for commitment?

Many view the world of marriage as the one place where a person can really learn about themselves in order to grow. After all, if all you do is date and have quick superficial relationships, you are really just acting. Your true nature will not need to ever be exposed as the lovers come and go. For some women, this state of perpetual romance and the need to stay non-intimate will be the only path to take. We should not be afraid of having somebody really know us. I believe that the dating process prepares us for some of the out-and-out exposure. After all, this person will see you in all levels of health, all times of day, in every stage of growth and long into the aging process. This takes your breath away, doesn't it?

It takes time to feel safe in this kind of dynamic. We need to have achieved some peace of mind with ourselves to give this a try. We need to feel confident with our physical and spiritual self. After all, this long-term partner will be the one to grow old with, aid us in the storms of life and comfort us in our time of need. Marriage is more about the hard edges of reality.

Remember that incorporating another person full-time into your life will be time-consuming and perhaps more than you were prepared for. If he is the right person, this process should glide along in an easy manner. When it is right — it will go fast. It is important to let others in your life know that although this may seem too fast to them, it is going perfectly for you. Confirm your confidence in the match. Keep checking your list for needed information. You have enjoyed the romantic journey and created a stockpile of memories and information on how romance can be incorporated into your union. If all is right, it is time to celebrate!

As you commit to this partner, keep some thoughts in mind. Everyday love is based on advocacy, respect, communication and commitment.

Wherever you are in the romance part of dating, keep these rules in mind. In the final chapter, you can review information and learn about some common themes in the search for the love of your life.

Chapter Nineteen

YOU'VE MADE IT!

"Never answer a question, other than an offer of marriage, by saying yes or no."

Susan Chitty, The Intelligent Woman's Guide to Good Manners, 1950

It has happened, it's happening or it's about to happen!

If you have not yet found your perfect mate, do not despair! Remember, we cannot control the timing. All your efforts WILL pay off. Hang in! Go to the front of the book and reread OUT LOUD the quote on the quotation page. Next, review your chapters and double-check your homework. Mostly, keep getting out there and it will occur!

Your time is coming. Soon you will be saying, "This is it!" You can call your girlfriends and say, "I've met him and I know that he's the one!"

When I met my husband, it did not take any time to realize that he was the one for me. I called my friend Bonnie. She had been with me on the night we met. After I realized that he was "the one," I called her and left a message on her machine that went like this:

"Hi Bonnie, thanks so much for the wonderful party! What a riot! Your food was great and I must have your recipe for the hummus. Isn't Jack wonderful? I tell you...I am crazy about him! He is so caring, so intelligent, so respectful, so generous, so kind, and it doesn't hurt that he's so handsome. I just know that he is the one for me!"

When we announced our engagement, she rushed over with a present. The package was small, but what a wonderful surprise. It was the cassette tape from her answering machine. She had saved the message above. Now, I had a record of my first revelations about this wonderful man who dropped into my life.

Review

Of all the information that I have gathered for this book, tw
facts remain consistent.

One is that there is no ONE way to meet this perfect partner. People have met on blind dates, in elevators, in hospitals, in bars at car rallies and so on. The other is that although each met in many different ways and under different circumstances, almost every one said the same thing: "I just knew it! And it was easy!"

Keep these in mind when you are struggling. First, you can meet him at any time and in any place. One second can truly change your entire life. And...you will know him when you meet him. If you have not had this feeling of comfort yet, you will! It will happen someday and then the process will be smooth as silk.

Dora was in a relationship that was so much work. She wanted to get married, but Thad was struggling with his career, had hard issues from childhood and really was a handful as a partner. They did agree on one thing - a church that they both liked. They respected the minister so much that they attended couple counseling with him. ***Scene Two****: Steve had been going to this church since childhood. He has just returned to town from a summer in Alaska as a fisherman. His first Sunday back, he attended services. He sees Dora and is awestruck. After the service, he can barely contain himself as he asks the pastor who she is and if she is available. He is told "No, she is not available now, but if anything should change, I'll call you, Steve."* ***Scene Three****: A few months later, Dora and Thad give up on their stormy relationship. Dora feels a great sense of relief.* ***Scene Four****: Steve receives a call setting up a blind date with Dora.* ***Scene Five****: Dora and Steve know on that first date they they have everything in common. By the third date, they are talking marriage. Steve starts medical school. They are married six months after that first date.* ***Epilogue****: When they find a minute to look back 20 years, at their whirlwind courtship, and all that has happened since, they laugh.* ***It was so easy and obvious when it is right!***

When I sat down to lunch with my future partner, I felt as if someone had handed him a script. Each topic he spoke about was one of great interest to me. The time went by rapidly and comfortably. By the third date it was clear to me that we were completely compatible, and I was amazed at how confident I felt about "us." I did not feel that tension and stress of "Gee, will he [illegible]?" and "when will we be getting together?" It just flowed.

[illegible]he women that I interview about their "great" relationships know **a secret**. the best relationships are based on two people who equally adore one another. **This formula is based on the comfort and joy that you feel about yourself! When the right person catches a glimpse of this, it is irresistible!**

Yet I still reviewed my list and listened to my gut. I focused on how I felt when I was with him and how I felt away from him. I asked myself over and over, "If you cannot change one thing about him, will this be O.K.?" I paid attention to the atmosphere when we were together. During silences, was there comfort? When we had a wild date, I still felt balance and peace. Was I clear about his goals for the future and what decisions he had made to get to where he was? Yes!

Most of all, was he respectful of me? How did he relate to my friends and family? Just because my dog Alex was crazy about him (she thought I brought him home for her), I did not want to overlook some important issue. This is the time I brought out my list and triple-checked. I racked my brain over the passing days and weeks. Over and over I tested my gut. Each time he was cleared with a 100% positive report. It was consistently the same...peaceful, loving, fun, happy and deep.

Don't despair. I just heard about a coworker's sister:

Kate had been going with a man for four years and they had set the date to get married. One night he called and said that he did not want to get married. He exclaimed that he really did not want children. Most of all, he did not want to talk about it. Kate was shocked and devastated. Thank goodness, she had not sent the order for the invitations to the printer yet. She wanted to just stay in bed and not go out. Yet her group of friends would not let her drop out.

They had different activities each week. The group went hiking, dancing, and went to the movies together. It soon became apparent that one man was really being attentive. He asked her out for dinner. It was so comfortable and she found herself laughing harder than she had in months. The minute the meal arrived, he asked her "How about a bite?" It was right then that she knew that he was the one. Why? She loved to take bites of everyone's food, yet it had been annoying to family and friends and especially to her last boyfriend! Right now they are planning their wedding in the Spring. She indeed is getting married this year, but to a different man.

Common themes

These same sentiments were stated over and over from couples who have met their perfect partners. They all talk about the following feelings:

- ❑ A feeling of familiarity
- ❑ A feeling of chemistry
- ❑ Feeling as if they known each other before, yet there is so much more to learn about each other
- ❑ A keen interest in everything about that person
- ❑ A calm comfort about the whole thing
- ❑ An inner sigh of relief, as if to say, "He is finally here!"

I know that this day will be coming soon for you. Until then I wish you the very best!

Defibrillator to give your heart one more charge!

Remember:

1.You have to get out there, but you do not have to do "everything." When you are clear about what you want and open, the Universe will do much of the work to make your wish come true.

2. Do not give into the heebie jeebies, keep optimistic about your goal. After all, isn't optimism one of the characteristics that you want in your perfect partner?

3.Have you released your going-nowhere relationships, have you completed your autopsy of past boyfriends and do you understand which illusions can be sabotaging?

4. Have you been observing the everyday miracles in your life and others?

5 Have you thought about how the "day-to-day" life will be after the dating ends and the real world appears? How will your current life change in both positive and negative terms?

6. Do you feel great about your life? Are you aware of all that you have to offer another person? Have you stopped feeling that you have to "prove" yourself to anybody?

7. Are you excited about obtaining your goal? After meeting so many men, do you realize that there really is a partner who has all their best qualities rolled into one? Doesn't that keep a perpetual smile on your face?

8. After talking to many couples about how they met, are you ready for that event to happen to you at any moment and in any place?

9. Are you ready for change? Are your life and home in order for another person to be part of?

10. Have you assembled THE LIST and are you ready to pull it out when the time is right? Can you live with the possibility of giving up 20 percent and are you clear about your non-negotiables?

11. Have you set up your Venting and Buddy systems? Are you

getting out with friends, keeping your numbers up and pursuing some interviews that are just for you?

12. Are you really relaxed about the idea that we cannot control the timing in our lives? Yet we can have our lives changed in seconds when it does happen. Until then, one needs to be open and excited about the prospect of finding the love of our lives.

What is the secret of all this partner attracting stuff?

- ❑ **Perseverance**
- ❑ **optimism**
- ❑ **clarity**
- ❑ **introspection**
- ❑ **activities**
- ❑ **and a whole lot of ENTHUSIASM!**

So the way to truly "Catch Cupid" is to aim your own bow and shoot as many arrows as you can in order to meet the love of your life!

Final prayer

Please join me in prayer.
Dear
Father
Mother
God
Angels
Teachers and Guides,
Please help me find my way to Passion, Peace and Prosperity.
AMEN.

WINNER'S CIRCLE

Marriage is our last, best change to grow up."
Joseph Barth, *Ladies' Home Journal*, April 1961

My original intent was to write a book exclusively focussed on stories about how people meet. It would have been filled with the true-life adventures about how people met their future partners. This is still of great interest to me. I would appreciate feedback from you about how this book helped you. I will send you a little gift for letting me know. So write to me!

Send me your success stories:

1. How DID this book aid you in your search?
2. After reading this book, and finding the love your your life, was he even better than you had anticipated?
3. Did the book speed up the process, make the process fun, change what you were looking for, surprise you in any way?
3. Most of all, I would love to find out HOW you met the love of your life. Is he an old friend, was it by accident, a blind date, at a party? How did this wonderful event occur?

My aunt has a wonderful collection of wedding invitations from the family. These are all framed and hung on the hall leading to her bedroom. It starts with the great grandparents, then her grandparents, and proceeds to her parents and finally to her nieces and nephews. The early invitations are done in calligraphy on white stock that is starting to yellow. Things get really colorful as we head into the '70s and '80s with niece's and nephew's invitations. It means something everyday as she finishes and starts her days.

I would like to start my own collection. Please send me your announcement or invitation so that I may add these to the collections. Also, send me your true-life adventure story of HOW YOU MET.

If you would like information about Trish's individual and motivational speaking topics, or to be added to our mailing list for current information and events, please contact:

CUPID PRESS
1009 East Hatcher Road
Phoenix, AZ, 85020
Telephone: 623-434-1679
Fax: 623-582-9171
E-mail: trish@cupidpress.com
Website: www.cupidpress.com
Books are available for seminars and book clubs.